To Heather,

I am so proud of the woman you have become. Your strength and drive inspire me. I am so grateful to have you in my life and I look forward to creating many more memories with you.

Your big cousin,

Amy Reed

"Faith is seeing light with your heart, when all your eyes see is darkness."

— Barbara Johnson

14 WOMEN SHARING THEIR JOURNEY
OF UNMASKING

The Woman
Behind The
Mask

UNMASKING YOUR AUTHENTIC SELF

Compiled by: Nakia P. Evans

Nakia P. Evans

The Woman Behind the Mask: Unmasking Your Authentic Self

14 WOMEN SHARING THEIR JOURNEY OF UNMASKING

Pearly Gates
Publishing LLC
"Inspiring Christian Authors to BE Authors"

Pearly Gates Publishing LLC, Houston, Texas

The Woman Behind the Mask: Unmasking Your Authentic Self

14 Women Sharing Their Journey of Unmasking

ISBN 10: 1945117427
ISBN 13: 9781945117428
Library of Congress Control Number: 2016953677

For information and bulk ordering, contact:
Pearly Gates Publishing LLC
Angela R. Edwards, CEO
P.O. Box 62287
Houston, TX 77205
BestSeller@PearlyGatesPublishing.com

DEDICATION

This book is dedicated to any woman who is or has ever been masked with hurt, pain, low self-esteem or self-worth, molestation, rape, feelings of suicide, spiritual identity theft, or **any** other of life's degrading experiences.

My Sister, know who you are! Stand firm in knowing you are the Original Design of your Heavenly Father, Christ Jesus! Your Creator has a purpose for you that is so immense, it can only be fulfilled by your authentic self! It's time to unveil the amazing woman you are.

Woman, Unmask Yourself!

ACKNOWLEDGEMENTS

First, I would like to thank my Father, my Protector, and my Provider: Jesus Christ! Without **HIM**, I am nothing. Without **HIM**, *The Woman Behind the Mask* would not be possible. I thank **HIM** for His many blessings. I am glad to be the daughter of the Most High King - and a spoiled Daddy's Girl!

A special thanks goes out to each of the Co-Authors *(in no particular order)*:

> - *Cheryl Peavy*
> - *Sequoia Gillyard*
> - *Casey Reed*
> - *Mary Reese*
> - *Tameeka Alexander Wray*
> - *Erika Hebert*
> - *Sherell Brown*
> - *Sherry A. Johnson Deal*
> - *Allison Arnett*
> - *Vanetia Fahie*
> - *Elle Clarke*
> - *Atneciv Rodriguez*
> - *Tamika Quinn*

You ladies are the **BEST**! This project would not have been what it is without each of you. I am so happy that God placed you not only on this project, but also in my life! I am thankful for the *Sisters* He has blessed me with! I love you, ladies!

A huge **THANK YOU** to the love of my life: **My daughter, Lyric!** You are my reason to keep breathing and to keep *pushing*. Words can never express the love I have for you nor how humbled I am just to be your "Mum". You keep me going and pushing every day. I love you to the moon and back!

To my Mother, Apostle Sharon Falana, and my Pops, Adetutu: I appreciate your love and support.

To my Father, Chris, and my Second Mom, Trish: I appreciate both of you, the love, and the encouragement.

To my Siblings, Caneesha, Matia, Destiney, and Dawson: Thank you for being my shoulders to cry on and vent to. Thank you for supporting me, believing in me, and always being there when I needed you. I love you all!

To my Best Friend (*you know who you are*): Thank you for being a huge encouragement to me during this process. Your love and support have been solid rocks in my life. I appreciate and love you to life!

To our Publisher, Angela Edwards of Pearly Gates Publishing LLC: Thank you for the support, patience, encouragement, and prayers. This project surpassed a simple business agreement. I received a new *Sister* in the process! Much love!

FOREWORD

In today's society, it is a very common practice for women to function in life wearing a 'mask'. It has actually become part of a woman's everyday accessory. If she was asked to be "normal", she wouldn't know what that looked like because she has become accustomed to pretending as if everything about her life is great!

Let's think about this scenario: How many of you have girlfriends who would **never** be caught out in public without first "putting on her face"? Yes! We all have at least *one* of them and, if the truth be told, there is a root cause for that. Now, I already know that many may disagree with me here, but when you can't leave out of your home in the natural state in which God created you, there is an underlying issue that is deeply rooted - and although it can't be seen with the natural eye, it's present. If we are not careful, we will one day look up and find our daughters have become us.

That cycle has to be broken - and it starts with **YOU**! No more hiding behind the things that make you feel validated as a woman. **GOD'S Word** validates you and confirms you are fearfully and wonderfully made, so whatever or whomever introduced you to your mask, it's time to tell him, her, or it *"GOODBYE!"*

That is exactly what this book will help you do. It not only provides you with stories of triumph and victory; it provides you with real-life stories of women who have traveled some of the very same roads you are traveling right now. The only difference between you and them is their **faith**.

> ➤ It takes *faith* for you to walk out of that toxic relationship and lose everything - just to start all over again.
> ➤ It takes *faith* for you to release the old and embrace the new.
> ➤ It takes *faith* for you to dispose of those negative thoughts that were spoken over your life, but you can do it because God says you can!

So, I challenge you to ask yourself, *"What does my mask look like and what does it really say about me?"* Be real with yourself when answering those questions. Only then can you begin to walk into your season!

I leave you with one of my personal favorite quotes:

"Every mask that we possess has a story that is waiting to be told!"

Will you allow your story to go untold?

~ Erica Michelle, Author of *My One Year Sabbatical* ~

INTRODUCTION

The vision of *The Woman Behind the Mask* was given to me to help empower and encourage women to unmask and be truly authentic. The word 'authentic' has been overused, to the point that many people do not know its true meaning.

My definition of being "authentic" is this: Be the person **GOD** created and purposed **HIS** child to be.

You see, what I have learned is that many of us don't truly know or even recognize who we are! We find ourselves being hidden behind the masks of situations that surround us. In essence, we have become products of our pains and circumstances!

The Woman Behind the Mask is composed by 14 different women - with 14 different stories. We have **all** encountered many situations in life, yet the courage and strength to unmask has been realized! Herein, each woman's account will take you through their personal journey as you bear witness to their *pain-turned-victory*. Today, these women *KNOW* who they truly are!

The Woman Behind the Mask

It's time for **YOU** to *KNOW* who you are. It's time to remove the mask. It's time to reveal the Woman of **GOD** you were created to be! When **GOD** created man, **HE** looked and **HE** called it *"Very Good"*. Know that no matter what has happened in your life or what someone has said about you, your **FATHER** said you are *"Very Good"*! You are everything your **FATHER** says you are! You can be everything **HE** has purposed you to be!

It's time, Sister. Unmask and reveal who you *TRULY* are!

~ *Nakia Evans*, Compiler & Contributor ~

TABLE OF CONTENTS

DEDICATION VI

ACKNOWLEDGEMENTS...VII

FOREWORD X

INTRODUCTION XII

TAMEEKA ALEXANDER UNMASKS: MEETING ME 1

SHERELL BROWN UNMASKS: THE WOMAN BEHIND THE MASS 9

ELLE CLARK UNMASKS: MAMMON WAS MY 'GOD' AND THE MATERIALS OF LIFE WERE MY MASK 15

SHERRY JOHNSON-DEAL UNMASKS: FROM OBSCURITY TO PROMINENCE........ 25

ALLISON DENISE UNMASKS: LEARNING TO BE F.R.E.E. 35

NAKIA P. EVANS UNMASKS: THE TRUTH BEHIND MY SMILE 43

VANETIA FAHIE UNMASKS: MY SON SAVED MY LIFE 51

SEQUOIA GILLYARD UNMASKS: THE COURAGE TO LIVE.................................... 59

ERIKA HEBERT UNMASKS: UNMASKING 67

CHERYL PEAVY UNMASKS: WHEN THE CLOCK STRIKES 12 77

TAMIKA QUINN UNMASKS: "911" 85

CASEY REED UNMASKS: LIFE BEYOND DIVORCE 99

MARY REESE UNMASKS: MY UNMASKED & AUTHENTIC SELF...................... 109

ATNECIV RODRIGUEZ UNMASKS: THE COURAGE TO UNMASK 117

CONCLUSION 127

UNMASKED AUTHORS' BIOS.. 129

The Woman Behind the Mask

TAMEEKA ALEXANDER UNMASKS

MEETING ME
Being Introduced to the Woman Inside

The journey of being introduced to the "Real Me" was one of the most rewarding and fulfilling journeys of my life. The process began December 23rd, 2006 around 1030 a.m. You may ask, *"How can you pinpoint the start so precisely?"* Well, when God makes a statement so strongly that you almost fall to your knees, you remember **everything** about that moment.

That was the day we were burying my mother. I was 30 years old, filled with masks of hurt, anger, shame, rejection, fear, doubt, and loneliness. I had no identity, no self-esteem, and very little hope or faith. Oh. By the way: I was a Bible-carrying preacher. By the time my revelation came to be, I had been saved since the age of 13 and preaching for six years.

Back to the beginning of the process...

I was in the hotel preparing for the funeral when the Lord said, *"DON'T LET A DEAD WOMAN HOLD UP YOUR FUTURE."* I **immediately** knew it was the voice of God, but instead of agreeing with what I heard, I protested His instruction. I began to verbalize to God all that was wrong with my life and how so much of it was because of my mother's mistreatment of me. I was basically telling God that I was *justified* in the anger I held towards her.

The Woman Behind the Mask

Well, God – in His mercy – let me get all of that off my chest then repeated, *"Don't let a dead woman hold up your future."*

That very day at that moment, the process began of unmasking roughly four years of pain. I already believed I was nothing, but the process reduced me to a blank slate in order to begin to plant the seeds that are now reaping a harvest for both myself and God's Kingdom.

I have no doubt there are people who want to read a story of how I was in a church prayer line, the preacher laid hands on me and spoke in tongues over me, pushed me to the floor, and when I rose, I was delivered and the masks were all gone. Well, I am sorry. This is not **that** kind of story.

This is a story of a four-year process of reliving some of the most traumatic events in my life. See, when we are being victimized, violated, and disappointed, we feel like we are all alone. We feel like God has abandoned us. It is then when we lose hope, joy, and faith.

Meeting Me

For the time between the end of 2006 through 2010, the Lord was making me relive the events that caused my mask. You may ask, *"What do you mean when you say 'relive'?"* Well, God (through dreams) would take me back to the most hurtful events of my life. I would see myself and I would feel the same feelings I felt when they happened in 'real time'. After I experienced it as I once did, God would then have me go through it one more time. *(Seems cruel, doesn't it?)* The second time, He would make me look up in the corner of each scene. It was then I would see Jesus standing there.

After each of the dreams, God and I would talk and I would tell him how I was feeling. He would softly say, *"But I was right there with you."* What that did was remind me that when I felt all alone and like God wasn't there, He was actually **very** present. That provided me this truth: I was not facing the trauma and abuse alone. That was the part of the process that lasted for four years. God had to remove all the layers of rocks that weighed me down before He could begin to plant seeds of truth.

The planting season came in August 2010. For the first time in my life, I moved out on my own – with no one to help pay bills or even go half with me. God was making me meet the "Tameeka" who was always meant to exist.

The Woman Behind the Mask

The first word that rocked me like "Don't let a dead woman hold up your future" was *"YOU ARE NOT AN AFTERTHOUGHT TO GOD"*. Those were the first seeds planted after the tilling of the ground in my life. Because of all I had been through, I thought I was created as some type of punching bag for God. It would seem that God would have said that to me long before **THAT** day, but in all reality, I did not have ears to hear Him because I was overly-consumed with all the hurt I had experienced.

For the next several months after the seeds had taken root, the Lord required of me to hear and research words He would speak to me, as well as scriptures. I plastered my apartment with those words. Those words were seeds to my now-naked soul (the soil). God had come through and tilled the ground, pulled up all the weeds of negativity, and used His love to remove the rejection, hurt, and shame. With every word I posted, the wall became a tree in the garden of my life. There wasn't a single room that didn't have words plastered in it. See, it was words that damaged me; so it could only be words that redeemed me. They were not words from another person; they were totally inspired by the Lord Himself. At the time, I named my apartment the Garden of Eden. At last count (before I moved from that place), there were 800 words posted all throughout.

You see, it is not about just taking off the mask. Many do not survive the mask removal because we fail to pick up our God-given identity and wear it with pride.

Matthew 12:43-45 (KJV) reads, "When the unclean spirit is gone out of a man, he walketh through dry places, seeking rest, and findeth none. Then he saith, I will return into my house from whence I came out; and when he is come, he findeth it empty, swept, and garnished. Then goeth he, and taketh with himself seven other spirits more wicked than himself, and they enter in and dwell there: and the last state of that man is worse than the first".

That means it's not just about getting the mask off, but also about letting God give you the identity you were blessed with from the beginning of time. Nowhere – **EVER** – in scripture will you see God identify us as weak, frail, meant to be in lack, destined to be poor, alone, or filled with anger. Those things are not meant for those who are made of God.

In conclusion, I want to leave you with what worked for me. It is something I use when working with others as well.

The church will tell you to forgive; I tell you to get healed. Let me explain. If you were in a car accident and your bone came through your leg, they would fix the bone and sew up your leg. For the next several years, however, you may have complications. It may still give you major pain and not heal properly. You can easily recall **every detail** about the event that caused you the pain. Now, let's say something miraculous happens and your leg is completely healed with no pain nor limp. You will be able to look at the scar and, if asked, you can say, *"I had a car accident several years ago, but I am fine now."* Now, let us apply this **same** concept to the inner accidents we have encountered. If you ask God for healing from those events, they no longer have power to control your life. You will find it easier to forgive those who caused the pain; however, as long as the wound festers and is not healed, it is hard to forgive those who caused the accident.

My prayer for all who reads these lines:

Father,

I come on behalf of everyone here. Lord, I pray that you would heal them as you healed me. Father, I pray that you give them grace for the process. Show them you were there for them as you proved it to me. Comfort them and make them whole. Awaken them to the glory or identity designed for them that they may forever walk in purpose. Amen.

The Woman Behind the Mask

SHERELL BROWN UNMASKS

THE WOMAN BEHIND THE MASS

Who is she when the makeup is gone
and the weave is out?
Who is she?
Do you know beyond a shadow of a doubt?

See, this question has haunted me for years,
Along with my insecurities and so many fears.

As a child, I was the different one;
To my parents, responsible – but to my kin, no fun.

I was always "fluffy", not the average size.
As a result, I silently cried.

As I got older, I grew and grew.
My self-image was shattered through and through.

My teenage years were not much fun;
I was the talkative but lonely one.

Graduation day came; I was free at last!
Here I was thinking life would be a blast.

Sure, I got married and had children, too;
Then my stomach just grew and grew.

Then the day came when looking
into the mirror was just no fun.
The only thing left for me to do was just run.

The Woman Behind the Mask

Off I went running – very fast,
But no matter what, I could not escape my past.

I was on my way to a heart attack
If I did not change my ways and get on track.

Now today, I am finally through.
The weight did not beat me...*I beat YOU!*

It was my humble beginning
that started this love affair
For potatoes and pies – I did not care.

My mother only made $96 a week;
When she put food on the table, you better not speak.

I desired cakes, ice cream, and chocolate, too;
But she did the best that she could do.

So, as a result of growing up without,
I made it my business to pig out.

When times were good, it was time to eat!
When times were bad,
it was time for something sweet.

What happened was I made food my crutch,
And emotional eating almost took me to dust.

Now my story I freely share
And gladly talk about this love affair.

The Woman Behind the Mass

We have to stop hiding behind the mask
That is found on packages, bottles, or flask.

Emotional eating is not the way.
Hiding your tears – it's not okay.

When we have problems, it's not time to run;
It's time to face them and put them under the gun.

See, the pressures of life can crush your soul;
This is why it is so important for us to be whole.

To you – wife, mother, and to you my friend –
We must put an end to this cycle
and in each other depend.

Our daughters are watching your life;
it's prime time TV.
Ask yourself if you're proud of what she sees.

If the answer to that question is not a resounding
"YES!",
I beg of you: Don't let food get your best.

I once contemplated suicide,
But I realized it was my pride that had to die.

Sometimes it takes humbling yourself
And just use that four-letter word: Ask for **HELP**.

The Woman Behind the Mask

So, if you find yourself once like I was,
It's time to flip the script and speak for the cause.

Too many are dying, children are left crying;
Hiding the tears and drowning their fears...
thinking no one cares.

I beg of you: Let today be that day
That you find freedom and know that it's okay
To be the woman you want to be.
See, I know – because I am finally **FREE**!

The Woman Behind the Mask

ELLE CLARK UNMASKS

MAMMON WAS MY 'GOD' AND THE MATERIALS OF LIFE WERE MY MASK

I hid behind the mask of David Yurman, Gucci, and Dooney & Bourke purses. Their value I thought was recognizable and undisputed. I believed that the more money I spent on what I wore, the more *value* was added to me.

There are so many things in our lives we believe add value to us. The truth is this: It is **us** who brings value to **them**. We often rate ourselves based on the things we have obtained, our physical characteristics, net worth, or relationships. Our *true* value lies beneath all of those things. Our *true* value is determined by the melody in our hearts. It's who we are when no one's watching - as well as the amount of lives we touch and help along the way.

The Woman Behind the Mask

I hid behind clothing, shoes, and money. I believed what I wore and the amount of money I spent on what I wore gave me value. I never thought about the cost of the clothing or shoes I bought; I would just spend. I love fashion and tried to keep up with what was trending in every season. I always had to look good - and there is nothing wrong with that, **but** it becomes a *problem* when it's an obsession and you base your value on it. I always took risks - and my fans loved it! There were people at every party I attended just waiting to talk about what I had on - like the TV show 'Fashion Police'. It was amusing to me...but it also made me feel important. I wrapped my world around being called a "Fashionista" or "Diva".

I would see people who I admired always nicely-dressed. I thought, *"They must have spent a lot of money to look that good!"* I would shop in the most expensive clothing stores just so people would see me with the bag in my hand. I soon found out I was the fool. Most of the women I admired were wearing what I was wearing *at half the cost!* Either they were wearing knock-off Gucci apparel or shopping at local clothing stores - and spending **LESS**.

While I was looking good and going broke, they were looking good and spending LESS.

Mammon Was My 'God'

I was on top of the world.

I bought all of my stuff.

I was to be praised for keeping *ME* looking good.

What happens when it is all taken away? What happens when you can't afford the clothes, the shoes, the trips to the hair salon? Who are you then?

Before any fall is the word "I".

I am reminded of the Bible story of King Nebuchadnezzar. Nebuchadnezzar was a king who had seen the miraculous hand of God at work time and time again. It was only through a servant of God that he was able to have his dreams interpreted (*his magicians and astrologers were unable to tell him his dreams, let alone interpret them*). He watched as God stood alongside the three Hebrew boys in the fiery furnace. He bore witness to their exit without so much as the lingering smell of smoke on their clothing.

Nebuchadnezzar saw the hand of God, but **refused** to submit his kingship to the authority of God. He believed it was by **his** might that his kingdom was great. God, as He always does, sent the king a warning in a dream telling him about his fate if he didn't submit himself to Him. Daniel interpreted the dream for the king and warned him to repent of his sins or be faced with having his kingdom taken away and be forced to live in the wilderness among the beasts of the field. One year later, Nebuchadnezzar fell by the "*pride of I*", and his kingdom was taken away.

God loves us **so** much, He would rather break us down to nothing rather than allow pride and greed to destroy us. Although God drove the king out of his kingdom, it was not done to destroy him. Rather, it was for him to realize that his help came from the Lord - the One who establishes kingdoms.

Much like the king, I became too self-reliant and independent. I forgot from whom my help came. The bills caught up with me and like the fall of a tree, "*TIMBERRRRRRRR!*" I fell down.

Mammon was my 'god' and the materials of life were my mask.

Mammon Was My 'God'

I was soon buried under a sea of debt with no sign of recovery. I then requested to be transferred to an island because I knew my employer would cover my living expenses while there. I believed if I got transferred, I would be able to save money so that I could catch myself seeing how my bills were being paid, but I was wrong. What remained out of my salary only covered my daily expenses (i.e. tithes, food, gas, etc.). **Financially**, I saw no growth in my life since the move. *Spiritually*, my growth was tremendous!

My shopping sprees became less frequent. The trips to the hair salon slowly diminished until they were all nonexistent. I would get so frustrated every time I looked in the mirror at what "was".

WAS a diva.

WAS fashionable.

WAS trendy.

Now, all I saw was… **WAS** a **HOT MESS**!

I would complain and my fiancée would provide financial support, but I had to use the money on more important stuff. Soon, I got used to the *MESS*. Then, one day I heard the Lord say to me, "*Give away all of your clothes*". I was like, **"WHAT?"** I didn't listen. The Lord **continued** speaking to me about giving away my clothes. I told Him I had given away clothing before I moved and that I didn't have enough clothes left for myself. Being disobedient, I *still* didn't give away my clothes.

A few months later, my church announced that we would have a garage sale. My Pastor told us to bring our **CLOTHES**, appliances, or anything else in good condition that we were no longer using. I knew then that the Lord *really* wanted me to give away my clothes because yet again, I was confronted with the same issue.

Sidebar: *You never have to question whether or not a word was from the Lord because He will **always** send you the message in different forms or through different people to confirm it.*

While I had begun my 'parting' process, I was not finished. My heart was still attached to 'things'.

Another sidebar: *God will always ask you to give up those things you hold near and dear to your heart to see where your love is for **HIM**.*

Giving away my clothing was - to me - like taking away my *heart*. As I began to take my clothes down out of the closet to sort out what was going to the garage sale and what was going in the garbage, I had to remind myself over and over: *Obedience is so much better than sacrifice.* I took the majority of my clothes to the sale, while another suitcase filled with clothing sat on the backseat of my car.

On the day of the garage sale, I watched as my $200.00 Guess dress sold for a mere **$5.00**! That really hurt me, but it also showed me this one thing: That was where my heart laid. At the end of the sale, I ended up giving away the other suitcase to a lady who bought the majority of my clothes. By that time, it felt like a weight had been lifted from me. I gave away *just about everything*, but God's command to me was to give away **EVERYTHING** and to leave myself with one set of clothing. *(I left myself with about three or four sets.)* I was **still** disobedient, but at the time, I didn't see it that way. I looked at the situation like this: They would be the clothes I would wear until God blessed me with more - but God told me not to worry. He said:

The Woman Behind the Mask

"Look at the birds of the air, for they neither sow nor reap nor gather in barns; yet your heavenly Father feeds them. Are you not of more value than they? Which of you by worrying can add one cubit to his stature? So why do you worry about clothing? Consider the lilies of the field, how they grow; they neither toil nor spin; and yet I say to you that even Solomon in all his glory was not arrayed like one of these" (Matthew 6:26-29, KJV).

I soon learned that delayed obedience is disobedience and halfway finished is not complete.

Yet another sidebar: *Whenever God requires a sacrifice from you, He always has a harvest on His mind.*

I thought I was finished, but God told me I wasn't. He told me, *"Whether you give it away or sell it, you have to get rid of it."* I still didn't understand what He was talking about - until I looked at my jewelry, which was my *second* heart. I knew I had to get rid of them, too. I took my David Yurman and Pandora sets to 'Cash for Gold' and was paid far less than my jewelry was worth - and **definitely** less than what I paid for them. I couldn't believe it - and neither could my fiancée, but he stood by me because he knew I was doing the will of the Lord.

After a while, the clothes I **did** keep became too small or tore until I was truly down to nothing. No matter how I tried to escape it, God's will **WAS** done! The clothes I didn't get rid of got rid of me!

I hid behind that which was expensive (at least to me) because after the countless instances of molestation I experienced as a child (*which made me feel cheap and worthless*), I believed that if I was able to purchase expensive things, I would buy back my value. At the end of the day, it didn't matter what I purchased or what I wore. I never felt whole. It wasn't until I found Jesus that I learned my worth could only be found in Him.

Last sidebar: *Your purpose can only be found in the One who created you. He alone holds the blueprint for your life. The only person who can validate your life, your value, or your worth is God, for Jesus said:*

"Do not lay up for yourselves treasures on earth, where moth and rust destroy and where thieves break in and steal; but lay up for yourselves treasures in heaven, where neither moth nor rust destroys and where thieves do not break in and steal. For where your treasure is, there your heart will be also" (Matthew 6: 19-21, KJV).

SHERRY JOHNSON-DEAL UNMASKS

FROM OBSCURITY TO PROMINENCE

I am a phenomenally-gifted lady whose life can be perceived by many as blessed, well-celebrated, and inspiring! By overcoming insurmountable odds by God's grace, my life has been elevated to a high level of success. One may ask, *"How is it that against all odds, she has been able to endure, rise above the ashes, triumph, and encourage others to succeed?"* It is because of my unwavering faith in God, an unquenchable intrinsic motivation, genuine love for others, and sound counsel received that I have been able to personally overcome challenges, break familial and societal barriers, and assist others with living a purpose-filled life.

Who is this phenomenal woman behind the mask?

Growing up in a poverty-stricken environment never lent itself to continual days of happiness. In the *grand* scheme of things, it **did** lend itself to perpetual days of economic hardships, fear, tears, uncertainty, and ill health. Although I had every reason to be thankful for life, those dire economic and living conditions oftentimes overshadowed moments of happiness. There were **many** times I regretted ever being born.

Beginnings...

I was born into a broken family structure comprised of a clinically-depressed and mentally-ill mother, an age-stricken grandmother, a brother, and an absent father. My mother, Pearl, always found the time to roam the streets looking for the next available handout and free meal - oftentimes talking to herself, spewing profanity at the next unsuspecting passerby, and engaging in lewd behavior. Sadly, she had checked out mentally. She had also 'let herself go' by never practicing good hygiene. The love of her life (my *supposed* father) awakened her love, impregnated her on two occasions, and then subsequently fled for the hills - never to look back, never to acknowledge me, and never to pay child support. He eventually looked back to take care of my brother *financially*, but left **me** to be an unnecessary burden on my grandmother and the state's welfare system.

Graciously, my grandmother assumed the role of both 'mother' and 'father' to raise my older brother and me. Although the role wasn't **easy**, she raised us the best way she could with the little she earned as a domestic worker coupled with the welfare received from the state. A strong advocate of education, manners, and respect, my grandmother's "iron fist" ensured that I was academically-grounded by encouraging me to pay attention in class and to ask questions when I was in doubt of what was being taught. She insisted that I join the library and frequently commented how along with manners and respect, reading a book "would take me around the world". She also reminded me of the Golden Rule: *"Do unto others as you would have them do unto you"*. Those words **always** encouraged me to share and help those in need.

There were many days when I often asked myself, *"How is it that others seemed to be exempted from hardships, trials, and tribulations (at least for the most part)? How are they able to experience blessings after blessings and miracles after miracles without major hindrances (so it seemed)? Why me? Why was I born to a mother who was diagnosed as mentally-ill and clinically-depressed? Why did my so-called father deny my existence from the very day I was born?* Questions like those bombarded my mind constantly.

Breakthrough...

It was at one of my lowest points in life that I decided to seek emotional refuge in the church. I **needed** saving. I **needed** hope. I **needed** to believe that life would get better. Although intrinsically motivated, *I needed the external encouragement to 'carry on'.* Fortunately for me, the church made me believe and thus served as an outlet for me to "belong" and "become" (so I thought).

In church, I was extremely active in ministry by helping others and, in addition, being the recipient of many charitable gifts (many times unsolicited, but gratefully and happily received). Putting God first and assuming my spiritual identity, I grew to believe I was fearfully and wonderfully made, even though others often reminded me of my physical flaws. Despite the low moments, I was encouraged and well-celebrated when I exceled. Not only did I find my spiritual identity in church, I also made some great friends who were considered family. They were there for me at both high and low moments. One of the latter included the untimely passing of my grandmother.

Opposition...

In my young adult life, I expected that sense of family to continue from all who had offered me support. However, now that I had become an adult, some of my support system viewed me as *competition.* The once helpless little girl - who had blossomed into a beautiful adult female, held her own, and attained success at every opportunity - had been despised by some of the very ones who had been supportive in the past. My successful momentum was not well-celebrated in the eyes of those who once viewed me as a charity case. Instead, I was seen as a rival and, as a result, rejected.

My life was a real and constant reminder that no one had **any** excuse as to why they could not have succeeded. If I, *against all odds*, triumphed and won, what was everyone else's excuse?

The once 'good friends' and so-called 'family' turned into bitter adversaries who prayed for my downfall and, at almost every opportunity (and to my astonishment), reminded me where I came from. I felt the rejection. I experienced the ill treatment. The hate was strong - a manifestation of jealousy, both stinging **and** vicious. I heard the words *"Who does she think she is?" "She has changed." "She thinks she is better than others."*

NEWSFLASH!

My socio-economic status had changed, but my positive and inspiring attitude never left, my charitable actions continued, and my love for God and others intensified.

What were they talking about?

Life Lessons...

By way of life's experiences, **this** *'Woman Behind the Mask'* has learned that your start does **not** determine your finish. The almighty God - in His infinite grace, love, power, and wisdom - can raise even the lowliest, marginalized, rejected people from the ashes, the dunghill, the gutter, the pits of life, and the ruins to promote them to a pinnacle of success that would *undoubtedly* baffle the critics, silence their enemies, and inspire others to succeed!

I also learned that the motivations behind *some* people helping others is for show, to have you beholden for life, and to make them feel as though they are superior to you. Sadly, some people are only comfortable with you and your success as long as it does not outshine theirs. They resent the fact that they are unable to dictate your movements, approve when and how you should be blessed (if at all), and to stop your achievements because they are too comfortable, demotivated, and lazy to achieve themselves.

THIS phenomenal woman now knows "to whom much is given, much is required". I have learned that those whose walk is not easy often have the greatest stories and testimonies that could impact and influence their spheres, the world, and generations to come. Life - the great teacher - has also taught me that if I wanted to influence and help others overcome personal challenges and trials, I must first be acquainted with their disappointments, griefs, and hardships. *How else would I be able to genuinely empathize if I have never walked in their shoes?*

Here's what I have discovered: Your pain is **never** wasted; it has *purpose*. You can extract the good from **every** low moment of life and use it as a platform to encourage others. It is there - in those low moments - when your character is reshaped, trust in a higher power is sought, and direction is revealed.

Know this: When all you have in this life is 'a hope and a prayer', you have something powerful! After all, who can better order your steps than the Creator of the universe? He is the *almighty* God, all-powerful and all-knowing, ever-wise and all-sufficient, and who knows your end from your beginning.

The Woman Behind the Mask

Your struggles and your low places are the pathways to your new life and your future ahead. When you understand the lesson in your low place, that is when you can rise out of the ashes to become the extraordinary person you were created to be! Don't be discouraged; success is within reach - for God can **truly** make *everyone* and *everything* beautiful in His time. He certainly did with me!

My success in life is the Lord's doing - and it is well done, indeed!

The Woman Behind the Mask

ALLISON DENISE UNMASKS

LEARNING TO BE F.R.E.E.

I can't say when it started. Was it my "daddy issues" or something deeper? When a car accident left daddy's side paralyzed, he moved back to his home country, Trinidad, because it was a better place for him to live. At the time, I was almost one and remained with my mother in Texas. I know she did the best she could to raise me.

Daddy was present in my life, but we had oceans between us. Although I spoke with him **every** holiday and birthday, I didn't *see* him again until I was 18 years old - which means I missed out on what I believe would have been some soul-healing hugs and deep conversations about love, boys, and life. When he went home to be with the Lord in 2008, I realized I had a lot of questions for him that I had never thought to ask...ones which **may** have helped me understand why I was "that girl" always trying to be accepted by being someone who others expected me to be - instead of simply being myself.

While being who people expected me to be, I lost my authentic self.

I didn't know I had 'lost' myself until I had found me again. I didn't know I was a caged bird until I was set free. I had always longed for acceptance **AND** more...to do more and to be more. However, I most often found myself constrained by the "what ifs".

The Woman Behind the Mask

"What if" they don't like me after...?

"What if" I get in trouble?

"What if" it's the worst decision I'll ever make?

My restraint was self-inflicted. I was like the horse tethered to a featherweight lawn chair, unaware that there was another way to live...waiting for someone else to release me with their love and acceptance.

It took me **over** 30 years to finally start feeling comfortable about loving myself enough to the point that it mattered less and less who else loved me. It took failed relationships, moving 3,000 miles away from my family, raising two beautiful children, divorce, and me losing myself in all of the roles I was playing to come to the realization that I was **NOT** being true to me. It was all a part of my process of learning who the woman was behind the mask.

It was all a part of me learning to be **F.R.E.E.** *(Fearless, Resilient, Expressive, Enough).*

I AM FEARLESS:

"...but perfect love casts out fear." (1 John 4:18)

I've been pretty 'scary' most of my life. What do I mean? I've lived by the book, followed the rules, and took few risks. People knew me as being 'scary'. I was called a "square". What was the underlying reason? *Fear.* I was *afraid* of consequences. I was *afraid* to push the limits - although I always questioned them...internally. Do you know that *"I always wanted to do that!"* person? That was **me**. I would look at others and think, *"I wish I was brave enough to do or be like that."*

The **first** thing I did to "push the limits" was rock my natural hair (before it became popular). Those closest to me laughed at me. My feelings were hurt, but I felt beautiful, so I carried on. Now, just about everyone I know rocks their natural hair.

The **next** thing I did to "push the limits" was move from Houston, Texas to Miami, Florida by myself - *without first securing a job.* I lived with my adult cousins for three months, and within that time, I secured three jobs and moved into my own apartment. I can **still** remember the freedom I felt.

The Woman Behind the Mask

Although the two scenarios were different, the *freedom* felt the same each time. I was learning to love me. I had casted out my fears one by one. I was learning to be **FREE!**

I AM RESILIENT:

"I never lose: I either win or I learn." ~ Nelson Mandela

Becoming *FEARLESS* meant I would have to make decisions. Some decisions were the best things since sliced bread, while other decisions bordered on, *"What on EARTH were you thinking?"* I took steps and could sometimes skate through life; other times, I would stumble. In all of my stumbles, one thing remains constant: I get back up. Some things called for better execution, while other things sent me back to the drawing board. In **all** things, I learned what I wanted in life - and what I never wanted to see or do again.

Moving back to Houston from Miami in 2011 (after six years), I learned how much my family meant to me. A divorce and two babies later, I learned the permanence of the decisions we make in life. Still, with all of that, I was **WINNING** because I took the lessons and built on them. Even though I still don't get everything 'right', when I fall short of doing what's best, I learn...I win...and I bounce back to being **FREE!**

I AM EXPRESSIVE:

"She's got bite marks on her tongue from all the things she's never said." ~ Unknown

I **LOVE** to express myself! My hair and style of dress are my expressions of my "determined to be different" attitude. Song and dance are my expressions of my "just got to be free" mentality. My choices are my expressions of my "live and let live" way of life. Then, I had an epiphany: *All of my outward methods of expressing myself* (i.e. cooking, dancing, poetry, singing, etc.) *are like parachutes for my thoughts.* They are the ways in which I could safely release my true feelings into the gusty winds of life.

However, I still needed to learn how to simply speak up for myself and say what I wanted…or didn't want - parachute or not. In all honesty, this one thing can **still** be a bit of a struggle for me if it involves displeasing others. That's when I have to hear, listen to, and trust that soft, peaceful voice within…the one that says, *"This path will bring peace to your soul. Do that. They will be fine."* Only then can I remove the muzzle of inexpression and speak my truth in love - and I am set **FREE**!

I AM ENOUGH:

"...and now I'll do what's best for me." ~ John Green

There have been things said (and done) to me and situations I have put myself in that would have me think I needed to be somebody else to be 'good'. I was always chasing the potential of "me". Always in a state of self-reflection, I stayed on a conquest to do and be better.

One day, I decided I was enough...right here...right now. Whoever disagreed with me could **STEP!**

There is a certain confidence that overtakes you once you realize just how 'enough' you truly are. **God** made me the way I am. **He** set me on the journey I call "life". **He** knows the way that I take. Every day I am growing, yet every day I am enough. Knowing that freed me to do what was best for me - all things considered. It's not a selfish love, though. It is simply *self-love*. When I learned to love my quirky, loner, overly-sensitive, taking life too seriously (sometimes) self, was when I could feel a rebellion brewing on the inside of me. It was time to break free of the cages - self-imposed or otherwise. It was time to be **FREE!**

I AM F.R.E.E.

I didn't wake up one morning with all the answers. I didn't look at the woman in the mirror one day and say, *"Today, you are FREE!"* No. It was a series of life experiences and lessons that taught me what freedom meant for *me*. They showed me what brings *me* joy and peace, because in a nutshell, that's what **FREEDOM** is for me: the ability to enjoy the process of being whoever I **choose** to be - *without* parachutes, *without* fear, and *without* outside approval.

Today, on the doorsteps of the age of 38, I feel like I can say I'm grown. Every day, I stay committed to learning to be **F.R.E.E.** to be *ME*!

The Woman Behind the Mask

NAKIA P. EVANS UNMASKS

THE TRUTH BEHIND MY SMILE

Alone. Afraid. Abandoned. Neglected. Dirty. Shameful. Those were some of the truths that were behind my smile. A smile is supposed to represent happiness, peace, joy, and love; however, for me, that wasn't the case.

My smile represented a piece of me that I didn't want anyone to see. My world that was once so colorful and full of life became dark and grey. Even though I would smile, no one would know the truth behind that smile. No one knew the thoughts, pains, fears, and abandonment I felt. I didn't want anyone to know the tears I've cried, the shame I've felt, or the many ways I contemplated committing suicide. I didn't want anyone to know that the young girl they saw who loved to read was trying to escape this life. I was afraid for people to know I feared for my life at the hands of an abusive boyfriend who put a gun to my head. I was ashamed and didn't want others to know that the demons of pornography and masturbation tortured me - for *years*.

The Woman Behind the Mask

See, some may know about my 'surface pain' of being molested at a very young age. What they don't know are the pains and struggles lying underneath. While it was easy for many to tell me I should "get over it", there were struggles I dealt with that no one ever knew. Sure, I would smile and make it seem like I had it all together - that my life was **ALL** together - *BUT* in reality, it was falling apart. I was hurting in a way no one knew. The thoughts in my mind became so great...so forceful...until I felt like I was going crazy!

There was no therapy. There were no conversations. I felt abandoned, left to deal with the pain and confusion of all that was happening in my life. I never experienced fear in the way that I did during that time. I became fearful of becoming a product of my pain. I felt like I, too, would become this type of person. My world was introduced to a demonic force too strong for a child to fight alone. *What does and eight-year-old child know about masturbation and pornography?* Yet, those very things became a huge part of my life at a young age.

It was apparent the enemy didn't care about the pain I felt. He used those opportunities to plant seeds in my mind and spirit, and for a time, it worked. My identity was **gone**. I became a *form* of a person I didn't truly know. I couldn't tell you what I truly liked or disliked because my choices would depend on the type of environment I was exposed to. I wanted to fit in. I wanted to be seen as a person who knew what she wanted, while in reality, I had no idea. The way I dressed changed. The way I saw myself changed. The thoughts, the feelings, the shame, and the regret was too much to bear. What many didn't know was that what they saw as forms "getting attention" were really my way of trying to find an escape.

That's what I needed. ***An escape.***

Questions filled my mind: *Do I take these pills to put an end to my pain OR do I continue to pretend my way through life?* Not much of a choice, is it? I became tired of pretending.

There I was in church - praying, preaching, teaching, singing…and living in a deep state of pain and strife. I was masking my way through life, pretending to be the opposite of who God called me to be.

The Woman Behind the Mask

One morning, in January 2015, I was sitting on my bed in silence thinking about some of the decisions I needed to make in my life. I got up, walked over to my dresser, and stopped as I looked in the mirror. I stared at the reflection gazing back at me. Even though she *looked* like me, I didn't know who she was. I broke out in tears because a life full of pretending had reached its peak: I was **tired**. Pretending had become a weight too heavy to carry. I needed to rid myself of all the heaviness that was holding me down.

How could I keep up with all of these masks? How can I continue to try doing things the way I was before? I knew *something* had to be done in my life. I knew I had some choices to make. I knew what I **didn't** need: another boyfriend, weed, nor another drink. What I needed was change. What I needed was **GOD**.

That very day, I made a vow to be all that God had desired and created me to be.

Don't ever think the unmasking journey was easy for me. They were some of the hardest days I could ever imagine because I had to face every single thing I had hidden. I had to face the pain I tried to cover and do away with. I had to face the hurtful words that were spoken over me. I had to face every inappropriate touch I ever received, every blow to the face I had endured, and every shameful thought I ever had.

The Truth Behind My Smile

What I learned during the process of unmasking was that I needed to detox myself of everything that was ever said **and** done to me. I needed to learn who Nakia truly was. I needed to find out what my purpose was. The only person who could give me that information was **GOD**. It is in **HIM** that I found the strength to endure the unmasking. It is in **HIM** that I found out how valuable I truly am. It is in **HIM** that I found my identity! See, I found myself in my Creator. It was time-out from tying to be a 'Knock-Off' when I was truly made to be a 'Designer's Original'!

When I smile now, I can smile freely because I understand the truth behind it. My truth is different than it was before. You see: Before, I was trying to hide my pain. Now, I am freely living and being who God has called me to be. Now, I can truly say, "*I know who Nakia is! Instead of trying to be a copy of someone else, I am the original design of my Creator, the One who has purpose for my life!*" I learned that in order for me to fulfill the purpose of my life, I had to become my authentic self! The truth behind my smile now is that I am my Father's Original Design, and I'm fulfilled just by being my authentic self!

Sister, know how valuable you are! Know how precious you are in the sight of God! Please understand your identity is to be His Original - never a copy! You are more than what you think you are!

The Woman Behind the Mask

I know the pain hurts deep. I know the words spoken seemed to crush you. I know the past seems to haunt you. Trust me: **I KNOW.** What I want you to know without a shadow of a doubt is that your past and the pain in it does not define who you are. Your identity defines who you are! What **GOD** says about you defines who you are! Who **GOD** designed you to be defines who you are!

There is no need to try to continue to hide yourself from the world! The world is waiting on you! Detox the negativity. Detox the hurtful words. Detox who did 'whatever' to you. Take it all and stand firmly on your story to share with others. The world doesn't need more copies. The world needs original designs to show others the way to go. I know you are strong enough. I know you are brave enough.

GOD designed you to be strong and brave.

GOD designed you to be fearless.

Remove the masks and become your authentic self!

The Truth Behind My Smile

"I will praise thee; for I am fearfully and wonderfully made; marvelous are thy works; and that my soul knoweth right well. My substance was not hid from thee, when I was made in secret, and curiously wrought in the lowest parts of the earth. Thine eyes did see my substance, yet being unperfect; and in thy book all my members were written, which in continuance were fashioned, when as yet there was none of them. How precious also are thy thoughts unto me, O God! How great is the sum of them!"
(Psalm 139:14-17)

The Woman Behind the Mask

VANETIA FAHIE UNMASKS

MY SON SAVED MY LIFE

"God will wreck your plans when He sees that your plans are about to wreck you."
~ Unknown

I remember the very first time I heard *His* voice. Afraid of how others would see and feel about me, I toned Him out. I couldn't let them see the *"real"* me. I couldn't let them know who I really was. I was in so much pain, I yearned for someone to comfort me and mend my already broken heart. I thought I needed someone else to show me who I was - or, shall I say, who I **HAD** to be.

I hid behind my smiles, my laughter, and my fantasy-driven joy. In that moment, I wore my very first mask: the mask of 'happiness'. I couldn't embrace me. I had to be everything **they** said I was. I became the woman everyone else wanted and expected me to be. My 12-year journey of living a life that was never meant to be mine began. I created a season based on my will - *not God's.*

Growing up without my parents was hard. It created a feeling of displacement...a feeling of no sense of belonging *anywhere* and to *anyone*. I latched on to love at 'first sight' and ran with it. My grandmother always taught me to seek God first in everything I do, but as a child (and even a young adult), that wasn't "cool". That wasn't the "thing to do" - and definitely not if I wanted to be a part of the "in crowd"!

What did I do?

I *secretly* allowed God to guide me - but based on His response coupled with what I thought my friends were going to say, I seemed to always make the choice to do my own will.

As women, we *yearn* for a feeling of completeness when, in fact, we're already complete! We just get 'broken' along the way. When God created us in our mother's womb, He created us with **everything** we need to live the life He envisioned for us. He instilled all the necessary tools He *already* knew we would need to be the women He created us to be. In every situation we encounter in our lives, God allows us to **decide** to do His will or our own. He speaks to us at the beginning of every thought and allows us the freedom to **choose**. The moment we get the urge to make a decision, He's there. He gives us direct guidance from the very beginning, whether we agree or disagree.

My Son Saved My Life

I forced a life on myself that God told me was not mine when I first decided that it was what I wanted. *"God will wreck your plans when He sees that your plans are about to wreck you."* I designed my own life. I chose the people - even if the people didn't choose me. When God said *"Go left"*, I went right. When He said, *"Go right"*, I went left. All of us can hear His voice; we **choose** whether or not to listen.

When I began my 12-year journey, the foundation I built it upon was already rocky before I added my building blocks of life. You see: In my mind, I was going to have my fairytale family life - one with lots of kids, a husband, a white picket fence with lots of land, and all the joys of having the perfect family...something I felt was taken from me as a child. So, in order for me to live "that life", I had to walk away from "my life". I let myself go so I could have the life I **thought** I needed. The fact remained: *That wasn't the life GOD meant for me to have in that season.*

I had the man - not a husband. We had a kid - and then he had a kid outside of our relationship. We were **NOT** family.

Over the course of that 12-year span, everything about me changed. I started living for everyone else - *except myself!* I became the problem-solver of everyone else's life - *except my own!* I had so much 'stuff' going on, I didn't know where to begin. I was fighting a losing battle with myself, so I hid behind the lives of the people who surrounded me because I was ashamed of my own life. I didn't have that fairytale family I made everyone believe I had. I had some good days, but most were full of sadness, depression, tears, and just wanting a way out.

God had revealed to me on several occasions that the life I was living didn't belong to me.

I was waking up every day with an **instant** migraine because I was secretly depressed and trying to escape my fantasy life. My most hurtful pain was the verbal abuse I suffered in my own home. I was *praying* that someone would come and rescue me, but that person - the only person who could save me from me - was **ME**.

I lied! I lied about **everything**! I was so mad at myself for allowing myself to sink so deep into my make-believe life, I had no choice but to listen to God. He let me go as long as He could until He had no choice but to wreck the life I never even had in the first place...before it wrecked me.

My Son Saved My Life

Truth be told, I was living the life most women wanted. I didn't have to work, but I did. I was stepping high in my 4-inch heels every single day, dressing to impress, hair done every week (*even when it didn't need to be done*), money in my pocket, and bills paid. Life was [**supposedly**] good! I can remember days when our family would make plans, but because I didn't look the way 'he' wanted me to look, I had to change clothes four or five times. By the time I was dressed "good enough", the plans were ruined.

You couldn't look at me and see the pain in my eyes; neither could you see all the hurt in my heart. *I couldn't let you see that.* The funny thing is this: So many women are living the life I **used** to live - and they don't **WANT** a way out. For me, I believed that was a sign of weakness…a sign of failure…a sign that I could never reveal to anyone. **Hell! I even fooled myself!** I wore the masks so much, I actually started to believe they were actually who I was!

I was **HAPPY!**

I was **SUCCESSFUL!**

I was **CONFIDENT!**

I was **BEAUTIFUL!**

I had my stuff **TOGETHER!**

I lived that lie for *TWELVE YEARS*! Why? Because I was empty. I was pouring into everyone else and not pouring into myself. I was trying to be someone I was never created to be. I made up my face and painted on a smile every day, just so no one would see the 'true me'. God allowed me to endure all the heartaches and pain of not following His will until it got to the point where He had to shut it **DOWN** before it shut *ME* down. It got to a point when my back was against the wall and I had to choose my life or the fantasy one. I was literally dying daily. God said, *"Baby, it's time to choose. What is it going to be? My will or yours? Reflect on what your will has gotten you so far..."*

My will had cost me my self-confidence, my joy, a child, and, most of all, 12 years of living a life that was never mine. I started praying and asking God to just release me, but out of fear and scared of what everyone would say or how people would look at me, **every time** He cleared the way for me to get back to 'me', I backed away. I was stuck in my own life, riding the merry-go-round.

Around and around and around I went.
It was spinning so fast, one of us - the true, authentic 'me' or the make-believe version of who I was "supposed" to be - had to go. I had no choice, so the authentic 'me' jumped off... and landed flat on my face.

There came that voice again. This time, there was a hand that I could reach. You see: I had to **decide** to jump off. Even though God was always there and I could hear His voice, He was waiting on me to **decide** I wanted to do His will. God will always show us the right way, but if we don't choose to do it, at the end of the day, we cause our own heartache.

It took God creating another life in me for me to start living my own life. My son saved my life. I knew I couldn't bring yet another child into a life that God already said "no" to. I had no other choice.

The Woman Behind the Mask
SEQUOIA GILLYARD UNMASKS

THE COURAGE TO LIVE

"Behind every mask there is a face, and behind that is a story." – Marty Rubin

We have become masters at pretending. We pretend so well that we have fooled ourselves, covering up what we do not want others to see. We elegantly wear a mask that outwardly looks good to the world, but we hide the truth of who we truly are behind the mask. Our masks bring us comfort. These masks eventually become prisons.

The only way to be free is to reveal what is behind the mask.

I spent most of my life hiding behind many different masks. I wore them hoping no one would see the real me; the broken me.

My masks allowed me to play the role of someone who had it all together. I was the star of my own masquerade. I hid behind these masks afraid to be me. Wearing masks became second nature to me. I portrayed whoever I wanted the world to see. The downside of wearing so many masks is that I had no clue who I was on the inside. I masked myself in hopes of taking on an identity that seemed suitable for the world, where I was trying to fit in.

I donned my first mask at an early age.

The Woman Behind the Mask

As a child, I was molested by two family members. I blamed myself for what happened and felt ashamed. I was afraid someone would discover my tragic secret. I desperately wanted to erase the horror of the violation but I could not. Nor could I undo what was done. So instead, I tried to hide it and pretend it never happened. I convinced myself that it was some nightmare I dreamt. Unfortunately, it was a horrible reality I could not escape.

I decided to put on a mask to hide my guilt and shame, to hide the pain of my stolen innocence. This mask felt like the best way to cope with the molestation. Because of my mask, I was able to bury this cruel reality deep inside me. I wore this mask so well that no one knew I was molested.

I felt safe behind this mask, so I continued wearing more masks. Each one was different. They became the makeup that hid all of my emotional blemishes. No one could see my imperfections. These masks gave the illusion that I was "miss perfect".

My life was anything but a bed of roses.

I grew up in a broken home filled with broken people. My relationship with my mother was anything but good. I barely knew her beyond her occupation as a nurse and her educational achievements. We were two strangers, who managed to co-exist under the same dysfunctional roof.

My mother hid behind her own masks. I quickly learned to hide behind mine while we were in each other's company. I often felt I had to step out of the role of child and step into the role of a parent for my brother's sake. I had to be there for my brother. No one else was. We were both short changed emotionally from our parents, but I managed to step in and give him what I could.

My father was clueless to the void my brother and I felt. He never experienced what my brother and I did because he was absent from our home. We settled for occasional weekend visits and child support checks.

It was hard being among other kids, who came from two parent homes. I am sure not all them had the perfect home life either, but in my eyes, they did because they had something I did not; fathers. I did not have stories of family trips or my father spending one-on-one time with me. I wanted what they had, but knew I never would.

I escaped the realities of my home life by diving into my school work. I was dedicated and loved learning. It brought me peace knowing the world was much bigger than the little one I was trapped in. I thought I could gain attention from my family by showcasing my intellectual abilities. I hoped by making them proud that somehow they would see me.

The Woman Behind the Mask

Being in an academic environment consoled me until it too became a part of my never-ending nightmare. The teasing and bullying I suffered from my peers during my elementary and middle school years shattered the comfort I felt at school. My peers did not know the hell I was living in. Their acts of cruelness contributed to me feeling lower than dirt.

A part of me wanted to disappear, but instead I tried to fit in with them. I became a chameleon, trying to shift and change into someone I thought my peers would like and appreciate. I had been a chameleon most of my life, so I put on masks to blend in even more.

By the time I put on my last mask, I was too blind to see how much damage it was doing to me. This damage opened a door for people to take advantage of me. My own insecurities started me down the path of people-pleasing. I wanted to make everyone else happy. Even if I was not happy.

I was an empty shell of the person I used to be, trying to fill myself with false notions that I was okay. Unfortunately, I was not okay. I was drowning in my own misery. In my life's story I was the caged bird, feeling incredibly alone. I thought I did not matter to anyone, which caused me to fall into a deep depression. I remember crying myself to sleep many nights. I was so hurt on the inside that I could not put into words how I was feeling. No one cared about how or what I was feeling. At least that is what I thought. My soul ached, and I hated my life. I thought I was dealt a bad hand. I kept wondering why God allowed me to go through those crazy situations.

I did not want people to know I was a ticking time bomb and ready to blow. So I put on my last mask, my happy mask. I wore a fake smile and made people laugh because I could not laugh. I wanted the pain to stop. I wanted peace more than anything in the world. The kind of peace I heard sung in Christmas carols a million times. It did not appear peace was meant for me on earth, so I thought I would find it in death.

The Woman Behind the Mask

I imagined what it would be like if all of my problems vanished; if I was no longer alive. Death seemed more peaceful to me than trying to live the life I was given. The weight of the world on my shoulders was something I could no longer bear, so I decided to take my own life. It was the only way I thought I would finally find peace.

I did not plan the how, when, where, or with what I would kill myself. I did not write a suicide note either. Instead, I went into my mother's kitchen and grabbed a butcher knife. I kept it under my clothes, out of anyone's view, as I hurried to my bedroom. I closed the door, took the knife out from under my clothes, and pointed it at my heart. My heart was where all my pain was stored. I thought stabbing myself there would release all the built up pain. I held the knife to my heart for a few minutes, thinking about all the things that hurt me over the years.

Suddenly, God whispered the words, "I love you," in my ears. It derailed the suicide mission I was on. I could not go through with it. I dropped the knife and started to sob. I sobbed for hours. No matter how much I wanted the pain to end, I knew that there was a fighter in me, who wanted to live.

The Courage to Live

As I looked back on my life, I realized I had the courage to live all along and face my hurt. In order for me to live an authentic life, I decided to stop pretending and expose myself for the impersonator that I was. I needed to be free from the lies I told myself, so I tore away all my masks. Revealing myself like I was standing on the world's stage and everyone could see my naked truth.

This liberation was the best thing I ever did for myself. However, I did not do it just for me. I unmasked myself so women around the world would know they no longer have to hide behind theirs. We are slaves to the mask we wear. I dare you to discover the real woman behind your mask.

Embrace your pain. Tear away your masks. Reveal the true you. Because broken is beautiful.

The Woman Behind the Mask

ERIKA HEBERT UNMASKS

UNMASKING
Saying 'Farewell' to the Old Me

In 2012, I was 5' 4" and weighed 160 pounds. According to Body Mass Index standards, I was considered overweight. No wonder I was tired and irritable! *Overweight?* I could not believe it! For me, that was the worst news **ever**. I was not the healthiest person, but I still took care of myself.

It was time for me to take a closer look...

BODY

Throughout childhood, I was pretty conscientious of my size. Many of the adults were overweight and unapologetic about it. They loved the skin they were in - and they should have! I must admit: I developed a complex about my weight for years to come based on comments from those same adults, such as:

"When I was your age, I was your size."

"Erika, you are too small. Put some meat on your bones!"

My grandmother had diabetes and always carried a candy bar in her purse - Snickers, Nestle, or a Kit-Kat bar...to be exact. At the time, I had no idea what 'diabetes mellitus' meant. I only knew she needed to make sure she kept something sweet on hand just in case her blood glucose level was low.

I was a single woman for years and years. I enjoyed dinner outings and loved margarita specials. 99 cents for one it was! Quesadillas and chips with salsa was my absolute favorite go-to food. Every Monday night, good food and good drinks! I live in the tasty town of Lafayette, Louisiana. *What's not to love?*

Once I married, that part of me did not change very much. I was not at "Happy Hour" on a regular basis, but I still ate whatever I wanted and had a drink or two.

Unmasking

Fast forward to 2012. I was constantly going to appointments: the dentist for periodontal disease; the neurosurgeon for chronic headaches; the breast surgeon for fibrocystic disease, etc. I was not active in any sports and never wanted to be. I am a supportive being, so sitting on the bleachers at sports events was enough for me. I have **always** enjoyed supporting others by being there any way I could.

One Saturday morning, I decided to do something about my health. It is very alarming to have breasts full of cysts (fibrocystic) and an occasional mass or two. I also had chronic headaches that didn't go away. To top it off, I was also dealing with periodontal disease. *Healthy?* **Not. At. All.** One day, I decided to take control of my wellness and do the things I **COULD** control. After all, eating healthy and getting to the gym a few days out of the week was easy. Me investing in myself was *the best* decision I ever made.

I am **still** in awe at times for making that life-changing decision. I never made myself a priority. I never put myself first. It has been several years now, and I still struggle with that, but I am honestly doing much better. I found out it is beyond okay to say "NO!"

'No' does **not** mean "Yes".
'No' does **not** mean "Keep asking until I say yes".
'No' means "NO"...or maybe some other time.

SPIRIT

There is nothing like knowing God is available 24/7. When I decided to go through a lifestyle change, it was the best decision - but also the hardest (I was 'that' person who did not exercise). Honestly, I love food. Food brings me so much happiness. I enjoy trying different foods. Still today, I enjoy different restaurants (I don't like *exotic* foods, but I enjoy new seasonings and other styles of cooking).

Back to exercising. The hardest part of working with a trainer was doing what she told me to do without complaint. I left the gym where I started and decided to work out at a training gym. While working out, it felt like I wore an "S" on my chest, especially when I surprised myself. Lifting weights was my muse. Being in **any** gym gives me a high I cannot contain!

Eating healthier was pretty easy, but exercising became a new world. I worked out at the training gym for more than a year. Within that timeframe, I learned to run and lift properly. I realized how important it is to exercise in some form on a regular basis. I prayed when training was **rough**. I also prayed when training was **over**. There were days I felt God was with me and that His presence was there. Sometimes, 60 minutes seemed so long!

Unmasking

"God, where I am weak, please make me strong."

"Sweet baby Jesus, help me get through."

"God, we did it! I thank you!"

"Whew! It's done!"

One of my favorite scriptures is Philippians 4:13: *"I can do all things through Christ who strengthens me"* (NKJV). I did not focus on one scripture; rather I read those that spoke to me.

MIND

During that time in my life, my mind was extremely focused on the goal. The motto at the training gym was "Keep your eye on the prize". I love that! Every time I accomplished something, I celebrated it. That is very important. Celebrate **every** milestone, whether it is losing two pounds or gaining two pounds of muscle. I always spoke positivity. You know that old adage, "Where the mind goes, the body will follow"? For me, I knew I could do it. I focused my mind on getting the job done. Personal development books and YouTube helped a great deal as well. They helped keep me mentally-strong. It is easy to talk ourselves out of doing something great. We have to give ourselves the 'food' and nourishment we need on a daily basis to enhance our thinking and overall well-being.

Now it's time to get down to the nitty-gritty!

Unmasking

I was very happy with the goals I set and accomplished, but I still masked how I was feeling underneath. I realized I was hiding behind my smile. You see, years ago, people would always tell me I have a beautiful smile. It was my best physical attribute. I had a nice figure and lovely arms, but my *smile* would draw people to me. It went well with my personality. I am an introvert, but my personality shines like a bright star when I am at my best. People are naturally drawn to me. Once I realized smiling would help keep me going, I smiled a **LOT**. Do not get me wrong: I am a genuine, authentic person. That is my true nature. I learned to enhance a nice facial feature of mine. I hid behind my smile for years.

I can no longer hide behind anything. I wear my feelings and emotions on my face. You know the term "Game-face"? Well, I do not have one. I wore a mask and had a wall built up that would not allow anyone through for so long. You were **NOT** going to hurt Erika! The wall started at my heart and went all the way up. It was created in 2005 after a heartbreak. In 2014, I *shattered* it.

Living behind that wall, I imprisoned myself for close to 10 years. That was **not** way to live.

The Woman Behind the Mask

Today, I am beginning to face every struggle and every form of sadness. I am creating happiness on my own accord. I refuse to imprison myself any longer. At the tender age of 40, I have a long life to live. I still have physical ailments from exercising. I believe my body told me a long time ago it did not enjoy weightlifting. While I wholeheartedly love it - and I do mean wholeheartedly - I have to do physical activities my body embraces while still being happy with the results. Today, my wellbeing consists of meditation, physical activities that are not hard on my body, and doing fun stuff. I am not where I want to be in life, but I am on my way...one day at a time. No weapon formed against me shall prosper!

"Masks, masks, masks...stories they always hold. A girl born Creole, African roots live in her soul. A song in her heart, much love and respect. Stories behind the masks, fascinates the world - imitation equals respect. It's in your color and hair texture that defines the physical you. The shape of your body don't compare to your mind; only limits you. Mind and Body, all the blackness men can stand. Melanin is in your DNA, carbon black sands. Black Diamond is you, priceless because of what you are. Infinite consciousness, wisdom, woman who endures all. Remove your mask, reveal and be that queen that thrives inside. Over-standing oneself, liberating identity, freedom be your prize".
~ *Bryant Benoit of Benoit Gallery*

Unmasking

Erika - also known as "Too Kool" - is fun, loving, strong, resilient, and embraces everything to come. Life is not always easy, but it is how we get through it that counts. Erika Hebert will **not** live hiding behind a mask any longer.

The Woman Behind the Mask

CHERYL PEAVY UNMASKS

WHEN THE CLOCK STRIKES 12

The occasion was a Masquerade Ball. Everyone was in costume with faces covered. It was a *beautiful* evening. There was lots of laughter and dancing throughout the night. A great time was being had by all. There were women dressed as queens and princesses - but **ONE** favored the fairytale princess, "Cinderella".

Cinderella was the life of the Ball. People were drawn to her beauty and energy. She wore a beautiful gown and dazzling diamond sandals. The shoes sparkled and wowed the crowd. As the evening wore on, she kept a close watch on the time. It was obvious to those around her she was anxious about something, but what? Well, in the invitation, it stated:

"At the stroke of midnight, everyone will remove their mask and allow others to see who you are."

As midnight approached, Cinderella's anxiety caused a mood change. She wasn't having as much fun as before. She finally said she needed to go to the restroom - but in actuality, she was heading out the door! She knew when the clock struck midnight, her identity would be revealed - and she was **NOT** ready for that! She loved wearing her mask. She enjoyed pretending being someone she wasn't. Cinderella always desired to be liked, loved, and popular. For her, wearing the mask was the way to go!

The Woman Behind the Mask

I want to tell you a true story about a woman who wore a mask for so long, she lost her authenticity. Through various trials and tribulations, she thought pretending to be someone else and becoming a people-pleaser were the only ways people would like and love her. The time came when she became tired of always pleasing others. This woman learned that no matter how hard she tried to please others, they still critiqued her and wanted more.

"Don't wear that outfit!"

"Why can't you do "this" and "that"?"

One day, she discovered who she really was and made the decision to finally take off her mask. By doing so, she uncovered her authentic self. That woman behind the mask is **ME**!

The Great Unmasking

Growing up as an only child was not always fun. I was often lonely and had no one to talk to nor play with. I was witness to many things that I kept to myself. From those things, I started to wear a mask and become a people-pleaser. It is not easy to share what I have been through, but it is necessary for me to share my story with the prayer that it can heal and encourage others.

I want to say that we have no control over things that happen when we are growing up because we are living under someone's roof and following their rules. Let me say this: Do not allow events from your childhood to hold you back from living your life and pursuing your dreams TODAY. It's hard. I know. We tend to believe things that happened in our childhood were our fault...at least I know I did.

My parents separated when I was two. They divorced when I was four. Then, both parents remarried. What a nightmare that was for me. I felt as if I was placed on the back burner. I lived with my mother. My father wasn't in my life as much because he had a "new family". So, every time I talked to or spent time with him, I *pretended* I was happy. I never shared how I truly felt: sad and unloved due to the lack of his time for me in his 'new' life.

The Woman Behind the Mask

One day, I witnessed my stepfather yelling at my mother. In response, she said she needed to "get some air and would be back". When I looked out my bedroom window, I saw my stepfather drag her from the car. At that moment, I wanted to run away - *but to where? Who wanted me? Why should I be subjected to seeing that type of abuse?* I remember packing up all of my clothes and planning to **RUN**.

I never told my mother what I saw because it was not my place as a child. As such, I grew up with a misconception about relationships: Abuse is a part of it! I never saw my stepfather **hit** my mother. Still, I was so mad at myself for never telling anyone - until now.

Being an only child, I carried burdens that were not mine. My father abandoned me. *Burden.* Seeing my mother abused. *Burden.* I came to believe I was the problem. In response, I became what others wanted and expected me to be. I wanted to be liked and loved so much, I thought being what people wanted me to be would make not only them happy, but me as well! I hid those negative childhood feelings and sadness from both family and friends.

My relationships during childhood and early adult life were adversely affected due to the life I lived. I carried that childhood baggage called "Not My Fault". I allowed others to disrespect me. I was quick to agree to do whatever people asked of me. If they were having problems, I thought if I solved them, I would become an asset.

I have since learned this: When people know you are weak, they will work it to their advantage. For me, the lesson came after doing more for others than they **ever** did for me in return.

I had (*note the past tense*) a friend who borrowed money from me. Her sob story as to why she needed it, I can't recall. When the time came for her to repay me, she avoided my calls. She **finally** gave me a check - that bounced higher than a rubber ball. She also refused to cover my bank fees. I didn't share what happened because I just knew people would call me a fool.

For a very long time, I thought I had the words "People-Pleaser" stamped across my forehead. That 'stamp' allowed people to take advantage of me. My **NEED** to be liked and loved so bad caused me to accept anything thrown at me. I was not happy living my life with others' expectations of me. I didn't know who I was. I would look at my reflection in the mirror and see a stranger.

The Woman Behind the Mask

My "Great Unmasking" was a slow process, but slow progress is better than no progress, right?

Almost four years ago, my mother and grandmother passed away - two weeks apart. Losing them prompted me to wake up and start liking and loving myself - flaws and all. God directed me to Psalm 139 that speaks of being fearfully and wonderfully made and how He took His time when He made and wove me in my mother's womb.

I made one **HUGE** step on the way to loving me:

I accepted my past. I embraced it as a lesson learned - a necessary lesson to place me on the path I am on today that allows me to walk in my purpose and help other women love themselves - without apology.

I lost a lot of "friends" when I removed the mask. I heard people say, "*I liked the old Cheryl better*" and "*She is selfish!*" I now have the attitude that states, ***"Take me as I am or have nothing at all!"*** I wore a mask for so long, I missed many opportunities to do some of the things I have always wanted to do. Today, I live my life free, happy, and 100% authentically **ME**. I have discovered I am strong and beautiful in my own way.

My message to you is this: It's time to **STOP** living a lie. It's time to **STOP** pretending to be someone you're not. It's time to **START** being transparent. It's time to remove the mask. The Ball is over.

It's time to *BE* and *LOVE* me!

The Woman Behind the Mask

TAMIKA QUINN UNMASKS

"911"

Mom. Wife. Daughter. Sister. Baker. Cake Decorator. Business Owner. So many titles, yet I didn't quite feel whole. I certainly didn't feel fulfilled. Something was missing. From the outside looking in, I had a great life! Pregnant with baby number three, happily married, great business, and a homeowner; but little did most people know, something was missing. I wasn't whole and didn't feel very happy, which was a baffling mystery because everything about my life was good. Whenever I would think about how I really felt, an overwhelming guilt would set in because there were so many real reasons to be down in the dumps, but my life wasn't one of them.

I had just made it to my 2nd trimester. The morning sickness was starting to dissipate. I wasn't vomiting every morning anymore. It seemed like my emotions were a little "off", though, but I was pregnant so that was expected - or so "they" said. Everyone said the feeling would pass. A time or two, I even heard, "It's just the 'baby blues'" - a term I had never heard of before this pregnancy. I thought, "*How could that even be possible? I don't get the stuff you see in magazines and on television! That's not real.*"

The Woman Behind the Mask

I went to bed on September 10th as normal. The next day, I woke up early, bathed my pre- and middle-schooler, and dressed and readied them for school so my husband could drop them off on his way to work. That was the routine - like clockwork. Whew! Uniforms, lunch boxes, kisses, and goodbyes as usual. That morning was just like any other morning...regular...the story of my life.

My every day routine was so monotonous, even my small children could tell you what we were supposed to be doing and when. Well, that morning, off to school and work they went. Back to bed I went; back to sleep - that kind of sleep that seems like the absolute best sleep. It didn't matter how much sunlight shone through the blinds or even how much noise was made outside by cars, etc.: It was the BEST sleep. It was the BEST primarily because there were no kids to interrupt - and also because I didn't have to share the bed or blanket with my better half.

I was awakened by a phone ringing. I remember thinking I was dreaming, but the ringing continued. Who could possibly be calling me this early? As I slowly answered the phone (in my half-asleep, half-awake state), it was my mom on the other end screaming, "Did you see what happened? We're under attack!" That greeting scared me so bad, I thought I was having a nightmare! She continued, "The World Trade Center! Did you see it?" In my confusion, I asked her, "What are you talking about?" My heart was beating so fast. I have never heard my mom sound so frightened. It didn't matter what she was talking about; it was the way she was talking with such fear in her voice that immediately moved me to an almost-frantic state of mind. Her desperation was evident. (My mother is now retired from the City of Philadelphia, but at the time, she worked in City Hall.)

The Woman Behind the Mask

I turned on the television. The news was reporting that an airplane had intentionally flown into the World Trade Center. I couldn't believe it. While still on the phone with my mom, I sat straight up in my bed and watched the report on the injuries. I was horrified, but not connected. In my mind, there was an immediate detachment - almost like a feeling of "Oh, how tragic; but thank God it doesn't affect me." Hindsight tells me perhaps that was a coping mechanism, but I don't know. *As I'm reflecting on that, it's amazing to think how easy it is to disconnect and detach ourselves from others' heartaches and pains.* The event was horrible and evil in every sense, but at first thought, I just wanted to go back to sleep.

I watched the live news reporting people escaping Tower One covered in dark dust, and my heartbeat slowed down. I wasn't in a disturbing panic. Then, right in front of my eyes and on live television, a second airplane crashed into Tower Two! My mother and I both screamed out in horror. I said, "I gotta go, mom. I gotta get the kids from school. This is war! We are under attack!" She responded, "They're evacuating my building." I immediately got off the phone and literally ran to throw on clothes then leave to get my kids from school.

"911"

I remember this overwhelming feeling of panic. I could barely catch my breath. I thought, "Everything I've prepared for in the military, I'm now going to have to use." On top of everything, I was pregnant. My husband was at work, so it was totally up to me to pick up the kids and get them to safety. I felt the most pressure ever in my life, but it was all happening so fast.

My drive to the school was frantic. I wondered why I was the only person driving recklessly. As I peeled into the parking lot, the first thing I noticed was there was no mad rush of cars. I thought, "Oh, great: I beat all of the other moms here!" I literally ran into the school yelling, "I'm here to pick up my kids!" One of the ladies in the school's office calmly asked, "Is there a problem?" "A PROBLEM?" I responded. "We are at war! You guys haven't seen those planes flying into buildings?" The staff seemed a bit unconcerned. I had no time to waste and was not in the mood to explain to them the world going on around us - the world the office of the Christian school wasn't privy to. I demanded my children immediately.

The Woman Behind the Mask

I continually called my husband's cell phone telling him he needed to leave work immediately, although it wasn't easy for him to just leave the bank when he felt like it. He tried to calm my nerves. He said, "We're watching the news from the breakroom. I'll be home as soon as I can." You see, he worked in the corporate office of Bank of America. He told me he had to get his manager's approval first, no matter how upset and frightened I was. Clearly, 'upset' was an understatement. I was livid! How dare he leave me to deal with this by myself!

Just as I made it home with the kids, I heard there was a third airplane headed to Philadelphia. My heart sank into my stomach. Emotionally, I'm taken back to that place. I grabbed my cell phone and immediately tried to call my mom, but for the first time EVER, I heard a sound I thought was only privy to landlines: "All circuits are busy". No calls could be connected. It was almost terrifying because I didn't know if my mom was still inside City Hall or not. I last heard she was being evacuated, but I had absolutely no confirmation that she was out. I remember my kids asking me why I was crying. By now, I had the cordless house phone in one hand and my cell phone in the other, all the while trying to get through to her desk and cell phone. No such luck.

I called my husband back. He immediately made the decision to leave work and suffer the consequences later, if any. I couldn't reach my mom. I didn't know what to do. Was it only Philadelphia having problems with the phone lines? I felt helplessness at an all-time high. I had some friends who had family in New York. One of my friends, Tina, was just as frantic because her mom worked near the Towers - and there was quite a bit of difficulty staying in contact there as well. I remember thinking, "All of her family is safe; surely mine will be, too" - but I couldn't even sit still! I was pacing back and forth in front of the television like a nutcase!

My husband - the rational one - made it home and tried to calm me down. We were living in our first home in Virginia Beach at the time. It was the kind of community where we all knew each other. We would argue on Tuesday and by Friday, we were playing cards at each other's house. I went out front to get some air. I felt the weight of the world on my shoulders. I remember our neighbors all coming to our yard asking if I was okay. I just broke down crying. "My MOM! We can't find my mom!" There was so much love, prayers, and well-wishes.

The Woman Behind the Mask

"Boo!", my husband screamed from inside the house. I went back inside and my eyes instantly locked on to the television screen. Flight 93 was headed for Philadelphia but had crashed before reaching there. All of those lives lost for no reason. My body felt like a teapot that had been filled with water and heated to a rapid boil. The 'burner' was turned off when Flight 93 crashed, but I had absolutely no way to process the pressure of boiling hot water completely filling my existence. I was scared, angry, anxious, relieved, and...happy - all at once. Oh. And pregnant. My head was spinning. I felt dizzy. My husband couldn't really understand what I was going through. I wanted to cry, but the tears were 'stuck'. After Flight 93 crashed, everything inside of me shut down.

I never said a word. The phone lines were still busy. I got in my car and drove off. I left the kids at home with my husband and didn't say anything. I drove around by myself for hours, then settled on parking in my kids' school parking lot. I sat there questioning those feelings I was having that totally consumed me. I didn't know at the time that September 11th would be the day that would change my life forever. I ignored repeated calls from my husband. At times, I zoned out. I also didn't know at the time, but anxiety attacks coupled with depression had been ignored for a long time. I had reached a breaking point.

"911"

I sat in my car praying for God to fix me. I hated the feeling, and that time was the worst. I was past the point of coming back to my "normal" self on my own. I was in a deep, dark place, even though I knew my mom was safe. Those series of events were the trigger - the trigger that unleashed a downward spiral of intense sadness. The sadness actually stemmed not from fear of losing my children or mother, but from an emptiness that I never addressed...an emptiness that I had become an expert at in covering up and hiding from the world. "I'm good. I'm always good", I would say. How can you have everything, yet nothing at all inside? I knew how.

God will save me. I know He will. In my darkest moment, even when I thought not living would be better than what I was feeling in this life, somehow I made it to the Emergency Room. I know God led me there because I don't even remember driving. There was a nurse who said to me, "Somebody's gotta be worried about you." I didn't respond for a while. Mentally, I was somewhere between the words I was thinking and couldn't articulate. My mind had been in overdrive for so long, the computer had crashed. I finally told them my name and phone number. They called my husband.

The Woman Behind the Mask

That night, I was admitted to a psychiatric hospital where I spent the next seven days. I was pregnant, so medication was tricky to say the least. I spent a lot of time in therapy. My parents came down from Philly and gave me so much love. I missed lots of phone calls from friends and other family members, but I begged everyone close to me not to share my "business" with anyone. I probably could've used the prayers… I certainly could've used the encouragement, but I thought, "They'll never have that much on me! Give up my perfect persona for the world knowing my reality is that I'm damaged goods? I think not!"

I left that hospital a different person. I had this "thing" I had to deal with now. I had these feelings of anxiety that would come out of nowhere. Sometimes, I could put my finger on it; but just like the sporadic migraines I suffered, the anxiety or panic attacks would come out of nowhere.

The next time it happened, we were at Busch Gardens. I had an overwhelming feeling that something really bad was about to happen. I kept saying, "Something is wrong." My husband said, "Meek, it's all good. Come on", but I couldn't move. As I began hyperventilating, tears ran down my face - and there were so many people around us. He got in between me and the flow of people-traffic to shield me. He has always been my protector. He pointed to a metal table and chair set, directing the kids to sit down. Baby girl was still in my belly.

He said, "Meek, breathe; you gotta breathe." His eyes locked dead onto mine until I connected with his: "Breathe, Meek." He guided my body over to the table where the kids were. He pulled out his phone and called the doctor. It wasn't the first nor last time my husband stood in the gap for me.

It has taken years of practice to master the masking of my enemy, my inner me. You would never know from the outside that I struggled with this 'thing'. The biggest and hardest challenge for me was the internal battle of "something is wrong with me" vs. "nothing is wrong with me". If I was good, why would I need medication or to 'talk to someone'…therapy? You know; that battle.

The Woman Behind the Mask

I wanted to name my baby girl "September" because of what I experienced during that time, but my husband refused. He didn't want to think about it at all. I did, however, stay with the letter 'S'. The only child who spoke to me from the womb; my Sequoia.

When we were all convinced she was a boy - even decorating the nursery in baby blue - she came to me in a dream. She looked exactly as she did at about two years old. Somehow, I instantly knew who she was. Without words, her energy connected with mine. She is my constant reminder that I chose life over death and the enemy didn't win. Well, maybe the enemy won for a little while because my journey was a dirty little secret. My struggle was a dark, lonely road that I hid from practically everyone around me. I wouldn't dare mention depression - that nasty 'D' word that secluded you to "crazy town" all by yourself. I've heard the way "those people" are talked about and shunned. I chose to keep it to myself, even when I struggled and stayed to myself. I have this "Super Power Mask" that will shield me from the world. It keeps me in my perfectly-shaped, shiny bubble, looking good when the world tries to get in...

Until now. The mask comes off so that someone else can know they're not alone. It is an emergency. As a Black woman, we can talk about the struggles of mental illness, and that will make us strong - not weak. We get to rewrite the narrative without the mask: The unadulterated, unapologetic, authentic you is beautiful and more than enough. It took me a long time to realize that. It's never too late.

I am my Sister's Keeper. Give love, not hate. It could save a life. Love saved me.

The Woman Behind the Mask

CASEY REED UNMASKS

LIFE BEYOND DIVORCE

When I started writing my story, my *intention* was to talk about living as a single parent after divorce. My desire is to encourage and help others who are going through similar situations. However, as I went through old journals and correspondence between my attorney and me, it was like I was reliving the experience all over again – and I wanted to forget it all ever happened.

The arguments.

The fear.

Even though I'm over it and have since moved past it, I found myself becoming very emotional as I was taken back to that chaotic time in my life.

The mind is funny. It helps you forget details of your life, to the point that they "never existed" - all so you can recover from the experiences. I still want to share my story, but only enough to help you understand where I've been and know what I had to overcome to become who I am today. I will share enough so that you can take from my story what you need to help you move on with your own life.

Signs. There are *always* warning signs... **"Slow down!"**, **"Stop!"**, or simply **"Move on!"** If you don't pay attention, you may miss them. Sometimes, the things we think we should be fighting for are the very things God is trying to remove from our lives.

Before my divorce, I was not very faithful in prayer; neither did I have a strong spiritual life. Ironically, those very things are what got me through it all. Although we tend to think we have things all figured out, we don't. We are not in control. **GOD** is. He **always** knows what's best for us – even when we can't see it for ourselves.

My now-ex-husband and I had been together for over a decade. We had been through a lot during that time. I experienced a myriad of medical issues throughout our relationship, including what I call "the burn". In June 2010, I had what the hospital called a "moderate" allergic reaction to a combination of medicines to treat my chronic migraines.

It was during my journey of healing and alternative treatments that I became pregnant with our son. (*My pregnancy is what ultimately cured my physical scars and healed my heart.*) I received treatment at an outpatient burn unit after my hospitalization and suffered through a lot of physical pain and changes to my body. I had scars covering most of my body, from my face down to my trunk. I had blisters in my mouth, on my hands and feet, and my fingernails and toenails shed. It took several months to get back to work and normal life, but eventually I did. I had a really great dermatologist who helped me get rid of my physical scars, but the emotional ones took longer to heal.

In 2011 during my pregnancy, I noticed things really start to change in my marriage. Life after "the burn" was changing. The physical and intimate aspects of our relationship were different. We had not planned on having a baby at that time. My **focus** was on recovering from my allergic reaction. When I found out I was pregnant, I was in complete shock and didn't quite know how to feel about it. "Kent" was excited!

The Woman Behind the Mask

As my pregnancy progressed, our roles reversed. I became amazed at the fact that I could grow another person inside of my body. I read parenting books and blogs, and bonded with the baby by talking, singing, and reading to him. I was constantly touching my belly to see if I could feel him moving. Kent soon grew uninterested in feeling the baby kick and move. He would flippantly say, *"I felt that already."* I think he was feeling left out and forgotten about, as he was no longer the center of my attention.

After Nicolas was born, I nursed him for nine months and took care of "all things baby". Kent and I agreed that he would take care of "all things related to the house" to help out. The transition back to work was a challenge due to the lack of sleep and being overwhelmed with new-motherhood, but it somehow worked itself out.

Kent did not involve himself much with the day-to-day baby duties; rather, he was more concerned with repairing our marriage. He said he thought I was a good mother – but "sucked" as a wife. He felt neglected with "no attention and no affection". I explained to him how hard it was to balance being a wife, new mother, and working a full-time job. I needed time to figure it all out. He never truly understood my position.

In July 2013, Kent's mother went into the hospital for a routine procedure after continued health issues. Two week later, she died unexpectedly. That was a very difficult time for both of us. Kent became **more** depressed and **very** angry – and he took it out on me. He never caused me *physical* harm, but the arguments, constant criticizing, and bullying began. The verbal and emotional abuse gradually increased as he fell deeper into his depression and grief.

None of my family or friends knew what was going on. I was too embarrassed and proud to reach out to anyone. It had been ingrained in me to **never** bring others into the business of marriage and to always handle things from within. As such, I endured the abuse and tried to 'figure it out' on my own. I soon learned to not argue back or try to reason with him, as doing either only made things worse. I chose silence. Silence became a way of life just to keep the peace. I only spoke to interact with our son.

I came to realize I could not help Kent through his grief or the repairing of our marriage on my own, so I encouraged him to seek help. I asked him to go to grief counseling and to participate in marriage counseling – or get a separation. I was miserable. I could see he was, too. He told me he didn't need "help"; he only needed his wife. He thought that I should be the one going to counseling so the therapist could "fix me" – because I was the one with the problem. Eventually, he did ask for help. I referred him to an M.D. The doctor put him on medications to help stabilize his mood, but that only proved to be a temporary solution.

When I realized I felt unsafe in my own home due to Kent's unstable moods and threats – to the point where I locked my bedroom door at night (*I would co-sleep with our son*) – I knew I could not continue on in the marriage.

God then intervened.

The week of Christmas in 2013, I tripped over a chair in our bedroom and fractured my foot...although I didn't realize the damage done until the next morning. Kent was away from home at the time. I called and asked him to get home fast to help. He hesitated, but arrived quickly. He helped me ice my foot and get settled. In no time at all, he grew frustrated with my constant requests, as Nicolas still needed to be tended to prior to bedtime. After helping with a few tasks, Kent went to sleep and I was left to care for our son until bedtime, even though I couldn't walk.

The next morning, we headed to the Emergency Room. After returning home, Kent and I decided it would best for Nicolas and me to stay at my parents' for a while, as he felt he couldn't handle taking care of us at home.

Kent helped me pack a few items for Nicolas and me, and I went back and forth for a couple of weeks to get other things I needed. After about two weeks, I guess reality set in. Kent's negative behaviors began to escalate. He was out of control. I contemplated getting a restraining order. I decided against it because I was afraid of the consequences. My parents did their best to protect us in their home. They would not allow Kent to come to the house unless one of them were present for fear of what he might do while in one of his unpredictable rages.

The Woman Behind the Mask

After a few months, I decided not to return to our family home. I asked Kent for a divorce. That was very difficult for me because it meant the person who was once my protector and the love of my life was now a stranger to me. He had become someone I needed protection from.

During our 14 years together, Kent never *physically* harmed me, but he did hurt me with his **words**. Verbal and emotional abuses are real and can damage you – but it doesn't have to *destroy* you. I am living proof: There is *'Life Beyond Divorce'*.

I am better, stronger, and so proud of the person I have grown to become. In losing a part of me, I found myself…my **TRUE** self – confident and unapologetic.

I couldn't have asked for a better beginning: **I AM UNMASKED**!

The Woman Behind the Mask

MARY REESE UNMASKS

MY UNMASKED & AUTHENTIC SELF

I'm standing in front of the dresser. The glass is shattered and there is blood dripping from my hands. Tears are rolling down my cheeks and staining the dresser before me.

"Lord, this life isn't worth living anymore. As a Christian, I know you created me with a purpose, but this life that is supposed to be mine just isn't worth living any longer."

Those were the words I uttered out of my mouth. I kept telling myself the pain was like no other. The flood of questions came:

How did I get here?

How did I go from having everything under control and a 'perfect' life to having nothing?

How can I move on with my life after this?

How do I take my next breath?

Think! Damnit, Mary! **THINK!** How can I fix this? I've fixed so much for so many people around me, yet I can't seem to fix **ME!**

The Woman Behind the Mask

All I can **clearly** recall is sitting in the living room with my son's father – my life partner – and our child. I was looking my son in the eyes while asking him, *"What will make you happy? What do you need right now to become the man you are intended to be?"* His grades had dropped drastically and he seemed distant from everything in life. I figured if I continued to buy things, he would bounce back – but this? This was different. He was growing up and I thought he was going through the typical teenage growth stages.

I'll never forget the look on his face as his eyes connected with mine. In his deep voice, he said, *"I think it's best that I go stay with my dad."* Those words pierced through my heart like a bullet. I felt like I was literally gasping for my **last** breath. My lifeline was leaving me – and I had absolutely **NO** understanding as to why. *What did I do that was so wrong?*

I did the number one thing any single parent does when trying to make ends meet and provide for his/her child or children: I worked. I recognize I hadn't been there physically, but I was there financially! There wasn't a **THING** I could think of that I hadn't provided for or given him – at least those things he truly needed.

I couldn't stick around to listen to any more. I grabbed my keys and went to the one place where I could bury all my problems, concerns, and anger: **WORK**. I jumped into my car and sped all the way there – just to arrive and hear my boss tell me some bullsh*t a** reason why she's about to reprimand me. Now my *JOB* is on the line? All of the hours, days, weeks, and years I had invested in the company – and I had to listen to someone who just walked through the door speak to me as if she had worked with me during the entirety of my employment there?

*God, this is **not** fair! It's **not** right!*

I felt sharp pains pierce my chest as I sat there. My forehead started sweating profusely and I started getting dizzy. I told myself, *"Just get through the day then go to the doctor. I have prolonged the visit long enough."*

The Woman Behind the Mask

Not only did I have to mentally process my son's desire to leave our home, my job was hanging on by a limb **and** my health issues were at a turning point. I was dealing with an auto-immune disease that people can't physically see – so to everyone else who looked at me, it appeared as though I was healthy, while on the *inside* of my body, I was fighting to keep up. I had convinced myself that although my health wasn't in tip-top shape, I could still do what I had done all my life: work and make sure my son and I never had a want or went without a single thing.

I left work and headed straight to my doctor's office – only to hear **her** say I needed to be taken out of work. I've never had to depend on anyone since being with my son's father. I vowed to myself that when we parted ways, I would never place myself in a position to have to depend on anyone but **ME**. In that moment, there was nothing I could do but break down crying in my doctor's arms.

God, WHY? Why does it seem like I'm losing everything I had control over? Everything was perfect. Everything was exactly the way I had it planned, Lord! I can take a lot of things but this, God!

Life isn't worth living anymore. Everything I've ever done, God, I did for my son. Everything I have ever accomplished, God, I did it all to show everyone that I was somebody. I had been a 'nobody' long enough since childhood. *God, do you hear me?* My hands are stretched out to you! I'm asking you: **PLEASE ANSWER ME!** God, I can't live without my son. He is all I have. He has felt every emotion within me as he grew within my womb.

Standing in front of the shattered glass – broken by my now-bleeding hands – and with tears streaming from my eyes, I dropped to my knees and told God, *"Please have your way with me! PLEASE have your way with me, Lord! I surrender! I've walked around wearing these different masks long enough. God, I can't do it anymore! I'm right here, Lord. Here I am, Lord. I promise you, God: You don't have to look anywhere else for me. I surrender my life to YOU – right here, right now."*

I knew that God had to make an example out of me. I knew He had been speaking to me for quite some time, but I found every reason to alter what I knew He was saying to me to fit what I wanted to hear. I had been running my entire life, trying to make sure I wasn't alone ever again. It wasn't until that very moment while sitting on the floor with tears falling from my eyes and feeling lost that I realized: I truly had everything I ever needed in my life. From the time God created me, He promised He would be by my side for as long as I wanted Him to be.

The Woman Behind the Mask

I had worn my mask for so long, I forgot it was up to me – **and only me** – to remove it. God had to remind me that *EVERYTHING* – including my child – were gifts from Him. He never said that those things He had given to me here on Earth were for a lifetime.

All throughout my life, for those things I encountered and endured (disappointments, hardships, and hurts), I would walk away, put on a 'mask', and tell myself I was healed. I didn't realize the very thing I had done **my** entire life I was now teaching my **son** to do the same. He was walking around with a 'mask' and saying those things he felt I wanted to hear. All the while, he was hurting and missing the one thing that didn't cost me nor his father a dime: our love and time.

I was so busy putting on a mask at my job and trying to prove to them I could do anything and everything, I ignored all the signs God was giving and telling me: **HE** was my only boss. I didn't **NEED** recognition from them; I just needed to seek Him.

The time had finally come for me to walk away and trust God.

He had always been the One providing for me my entire life. He wouldn't stop doing so now! I was and could be nothing to anyone around me if I was no longer here on Earth. God said our body is our temple and we must take care of it.

I realized that those things I accomplished, gained, or achieved meant nothing to the **ONLY** person in my life who loved me unconditionally: My Father God, My Jehovah Jireh – my Provider, My Daddy – the Beginning and the End.

I now walk around unmasked and am my authentic self. I am who **God** created me to be, for there is no greater feeling than to learn to love yourself wholeheartedly – and to know you are loved in return by Him.

The Woman Behind the Mask
ATNECIV RODRIGUEZ UNMASKS

THE COURAGE TO UNMASK

"Courage is the ability to make decisions and hold them in the face of fear." ~ Unknown

Having been through so much in my life, I'd like to share how I have been able to overcome so much while in the process of growing through personal development. My name is Atneciv. People call me 'Nessy'. As a product of my environment, it seemed as if I was destined to be a single mom "in the hood". I grew up in a family that had little to no ambition to progress in life. I had many dreams and was gifted with many talents; however, I wasn't pushed by my family to go after those dreams and goals. My father passed away when I was three years old, which left me without a positive male figure in my life.

When I was eight, I was molested by someone who was supposed to be trusted. That was the beginning of fear and the end of trust. I witnessed my mom being abused by that same man. She eventually left him, but she didn't recognize I was a child with issues - ones that were not revealed until later on in my life, as I didn't speak up about them until I was older.

For a good portion of my early life, I was an only child. I had a sister who passed away, and my little brother wasn't born until I was 14. Being an only child wasn't bad. My mom tried to make the best of things, even though we struggled. Growing up alone taught me loneliness. I learned to hustle like my mom because she always taught me not to depend on a man. For many years, she was single. To me, that became the norm.

Fast-forward to my teenage years. I struggled in school. Of course, I only wanted to hang out, but my mom was quite strict. My troubled self went about my business and became this promiscuous girl. At age 16, my promiscuity led me to birth my first child; at the age of 17, I had my second. I had no idea how I was going manage life with two children, but I went about my life doing what I had to do.

My first major accomplishment was graduating high school. No one really ever thought I would finish, but I did. Deep down, I needed to prove everyone wrong who thought less of me. That was a great feeling - one that resonated with me for a long time. While I thought I had it all together at that point, my self-esteem was being destroyed by the father of my children. He was the "bad boy" all the girls wanted. He had been in and out of the juvenile detention system several times. He drank liquor, and I happened to think that was cool. He began to be abusive towards me.

Remember: That was my norm. Seventeen years old with two children and in an abusive relationship.

I had no way out. With both fear and love in my mind, I actually didn't want out. I wanted him so bad, and in my mind, I was going to be with him through thick and thin. Things got so bad, he was using drugs and drinking alcohol every single day. The physical fights got worse, too. The fear he instilled in me was unexplainable. No matter how many marks I had on me from his abuse, I would still cover them up and deny to 'the world' there was anything wrong.

My mother was no stranger to that type of abuse. I knew deep down she tried to help me, but I would not budge - until I one day caught him cheating. That was the day I felt my world turn upside down. He left me after everything I did for him, yet I still loved him. That year was very difficult for me. I thought I was going to be with him forever. After all, we had two children! I was able to move past that chapter in my life, and I thank God I left because it was a matter of life or death.

The Woman Behind the Mask

I was 21 years old with no life ambition and living in the projects. I began to find myself. I was hanging out with friends, found jobs here and there, and, while things were going great, I found someone. At the time, I was VERY confident. He was, too, but my mentality was still the same. He was tough and gave me so much attention. He was fun and said the things I wanted to hear. He played with my children and they enjoyed his company as well. I often worried about being single like my mom. I wanted to break that cycle. I felt good with him. He was a "protector" - as I called him. We soon moved in together and before I knew it, I was pregnant with my third child.

Little by little, I started seeing changes. He became obsessive. He hated my BFF (Best Friend Forever), and things happened so quickly between he and I that my BFF and I became distant. He didn't have a job, but who was I to judge? At the time, I didn't have a job either. He accused me of being unfaithful regularly. We began arguing and that progressed into physical abuse as well. He became a total jerk to my children.

The Courage to Unmask

When I had our baby, things changed drastically. He was not the guy he said he was. I still remained hopeful because I didn't want to have another relationship or have fatherless children. The relationship was so detrimental. The emotional abuse was sometimes worse, as my life and identity were being chipped away. I no longer had the confidence I once possessed and lost control of my life once again; I still remained hopeful. I imagined things would one day go back to how they used to be when we were all happy. I pretended to be the perfect partner when in public. We were "the ideal couple". Behind closed doors, the fear, pain, and suffering were my reality.

Years passed and I was the main breadwinner. He would have seasonal jobs, but they wouldn't help sustain the family. We had some good times, though. It was during one of those "honeymoon phases" that I married him. I thought things would get better. I worked; he tried to work. Then, I decided to start making a change. The life I was living was not exactly what I wanted. I wasn't trying to keep up with the Joneses, but my life was leading nowhere.

The Woman Behind the Mask

I decided to go to school to get a higher-education degree. He hated that and, with caution, I explained that it was to help us. I began working with nonprofit organizations where the missions were to help others - something that has always been a passion of mine. He hated that, too, and again (with caution), I explained I had to work. One day, after obtaining my first degree, I landed a job as a Domestic Violence Counselor. That was my turning point. You guessed it: He hated that, too!

The job saved me. I learned so much from the training alone. I then began speaking to women and helped them with resources. The more they spoke to me about their issues, the more I realized, "These women are telling my story!" I learned the dynamics of abuse, the effects on children, social effects, and so much more.

Meanwhile, back at home, our relationship grew worse. I fully resented him. Then, no matter how afraid of change I was, I finally took the leap of faith and left him. We went through several breakups during the course of our relationship, but nothing like that final one. Three restraining orders and three breakups later, we were officially separated. Truth be told, when we divorced, I was still in love with him - but I knew he was never going to change. There was nothing more I wanted than for us to grow. I wanted it, but he didn't. I could no longer stand the emotional abuse the children and I were enduring. During the divorce, I started an MLM business, graduated with a Bachelor's Degree, and made the decision to empower women outside of my work environment. That was my therapy, my breakthrough, and my unmasking.

I began to live life on purpose. Getting a grasp on life wasn't easy. I'm still developing into the woman I want to be. Personal development has been a great journey, and I make it a daily priority. I find so much fulfillment in teaching women a healthy way of life. I have helped so many families within my own journey, and it has been a blessing. God has blessed me.

The Woman Behind the Mask

Can I say I was destined to be a single mother? Yes. For now. It's not necessarily a bad thing. God does things on purpose. I was meant to go down this path so that I can help others unmask their true selves. Women's empowerment has been a healing source for me. I was always a happy person and held a smile everywhere I went, but I could only do so much smiling before the frown behind my mask started to show - and believe me: people know.

Let me leave you with a few tips - ones that will help you in the process of unmasking:

#UnmaskingTips

1. Don't wait until you can no longer deal with the internal battles. Stress will literally break you down both physically and emotionally.

2. Go after what you want and be true to yourself. Let go of anything that is toxic to your happiness and well-being, even if you are scared to death.

3. Ask yourself, "What am I willing to do or go through in order to live a happy, fulfilling life?"

4. Begin to switch your mindset and uncover yourself from disbelief. You are who you choose to be, and I promise you can recreate your blueprint into the person you want. The courage it took to unmask myself was hard, but sometimes it hurts getting through the process in order to get where you need to be.

5. Gain the courage and throw away the mask! Look in the mirror and take a look at the new unmasked you!

Taking a courageous step really means you have to get out of your comfort zone. It's a process that doesn't happen overnight, but little courageous steps will help you get there. I wasn't who I am today from one decision; it was an accumulation of decisions that molded my family and continues to mold my future.

You can find your true self when you begin to accept the value of who you are, flaws and all! XOX

CONCLUSION

We pray you have enjoyed our stories. We also hope and pray that along this journey of reading the stories, you were encouraged to know your *Spiritual Identity* and be all that God has for you to be! **Never** forget who you are and who you belong to!

Take the stories you have read - along with the information gathered - and start living...*today*. Live authentically, just as God created you to do! Never live below your purpose. Be the great woman He has destined you to be. Don't allow anyone to stop your **shine**!

Unmask and live AUTHENTICALLY!

UNMASKED AUTHORS' BIOS

Nakia P. Evans, The Authentic Living Strategist, is the Founder/CEO of *Authentically You* and *Authentically You Magazine*. She is also the Radio Host of *Real Talk with Kia Radio, Ladies Table Talk*. After dealing with many struggles in her life, Nakia knows what it feels like to be masked, covered, hidden, and abandoned. It is her passion and vision to help empower women to embrace who they truly are and for them to know what their Father and Creator has said about them! Nakia helps women unmask and face those things that are hindering them by empowering them to unveil their true selves to the world! She lives in Camden, South Carolina with her daughter, Lyric. Connect with Nakia at:

Facebook: FearfullyMade2
Facebook Group:
facebook.com/groups/538442416343461
Web: www.authenticallymagazine.com
Instagram: nakia_evans1
Twitter: nakia_evans1

Unmasked Authors' Bios

Tameeka Alexander-Wray is the daughter of Pastor Roosevelt Alexander and Alice Alexander. Tameeka accepted the call to ministry in November 2000. She is currently the Assistant Pastor at Freedom Christian Assembly and is the Founder of Prophet of Life Ministries. She holds a BS Degree in Criminal Justice from Morris College. She is a Captain with the South Carolina Department of Juvenile Justice. In May 2016, the Lord birthed *Women at the Well* through Prophet Tameeka. She is married to Bro. Jarrod Wray, and in 2014, they became the parents of Eden Morning.

Connect with her on Facebook at
Tameeka Alexander Wray
or via email at
Prophetic.Teacher01@gmail.com

The Woman Behind the Mask

Sherell Brown is a Category Creator in the Health and Wellness arena by combining a mix of both professional skills and personal experiences that produces results. She is the C.E.O. of Sherell Brown Health Concierge Services, the Publisher of *L.O.S.E. Health & Wellness Magazine*, the Host of the talk show "Ask Sherell" and Author of *The Blueprint To Weight Loss: The Truth Revealed*. She has spearheaded campaigns such as "The Bra Out", a fundraiser designed to bring awareness to Breast Cancer in the Island of Abaco, Bahamas. She is the Founder of The War Against Obesity The Cause where she is teaching people how to eat to live and not to die! She also offers limited personal coaching and consulting. Sherell presently lives in Murfreesboro, TN with her husband, Desmond Brown, and her two children, young Master Seth and Princess Grace Brown. With her love for the Lord and her relentless passion, Sherell is ready to serve you.

Unmasked Authors' Bios

Elle Clarke is the C.E.O. of Elle Clarke Media Group. She is an Author, a Motivational Speaker & Coach, and the Founder of "I Am Queen: The Movement". Known as the 'Encourager', Elle is a Sexual Violence Expert. She served as a Detective for 12 years until July 2015 when she decided to retire to pursue her purpose. She has also survived her own story of molestation and rape and now helps women overcome the hurt of their past, transform their pain into profit, and embrace the Queen within. Elle is a Contributing Writer for the Huffington Post, the Author of *How I Escaped the Prison of Rape*, and a Contributing Author for *The Woman Behind the Mask*. Connect with Elle at:

Web: www.elleclarke.com
Facebook: Heiress Elle Clarke
Facebook Group: I Am Queen: The Movement
Facebook: Elle Clarke
Instagram: Heiresselle Clarke

The Woman Behind the Mask

Sherry Johnson-Deal is a phenomenally gifted woman, a trailblazer, and undoubtedly a natural born leader; one who has made tremendous strides in all areas of life by overcoming insurmountable odds and inspiring others to live their dreams. A diplomat by profession and one who exudes a spirit of excellence and perseverance, she does her best in whatever assignment given and never gives up! At present, she is the Editor of *L.O.S.E. E-fitness and Wellness Magazine* and Editor of several books, including the recently published *The Blueprint to Weight Loss: The Truth Exposed* by Sherell Brown. She is in the process of pursuing purpose by rebranding herself as a Life Coach, Counselor, Talk Show Host, Author, and Media Mogul. Connect with Sherry at:

Email: sherryann.johnsondeal@gmail.com
Twitter: SAnnJD
LinkedIn: Sherry A Johnson Deal
Instagram: sherryjohnsondeal
Periscope: Sherry Johnson-Deal
Skype: Sherry Johnson-Deal

Allison Denise, affectionately known as "The Creative Accountant", is a multi-passionate girl-boss who loves when her purpose meets her pennies - and even more so when everything's pretty! She enjoys using her experience of 18 years in Accounting and seven years in Graphic Design to share tips, information, and affirmations on how other DIY Fempreneurs can keep their coins in check and their brand beautiful! When not designing websites and Speaker Sheets, you can find her encouraging others and loving on her family.

Connect with her on Social Media at
ImAllisonDenise.
Learn more about her services and courses by
visiting www.ImAllisonDenise.com

The Woman Behind the Mask

Vanetia Fahie, "The Experience Architect", is on a journey to Renewing the SHE IN YOU, and being Fierce, Fabulous, and Fearless while having Intentional Success. She is the Founder, President/C.E.O. of the DO YOU Enrichment Center and Founder/SHE-E.O. of La Femme & *La Femme Magazine*. Vanetia is the single mom of Zoriah Heyward and Denode Heyward, Jr., and is passionate about helping other single moms rediscover the SHE that lives within her. She stands firmly on the belief that if you divorce your fears and marry your strength, your life will change! Connect with Venetia at:

Web: www.lafemme-inc.com
Facebook: maglafemme
Instagram: maglafemme
Twitter: maglafemme

Unmasked Authors' Bios

Sequoia Gillyard, The Word Worshiper, is Editor-in-Chief of *Rejoicing Hope Magazine*. She is also a writer for the Huffington Post. She reaches straight into the souls of every audience through powerful spoken and written words, uplifting them to imagine and experience new levels of greatness.

A poet, speaker, actress, and the author of *Pillars of Hope*, Sequoia is known for her ability to help women who are lost, hurting, and suffering in silence. Sequoia's style is warm, authentic, and transparent. She firmly believes that lives can be changed and even saved through positive words that speak life. Connect with Sequoia at:

Facebook: Sequoia T. Gillyard
Twitter: SequoiaConquers
Instagram: SequoiaGillyard
Web: www.sequoiatgillyard.com

The Woman Behind the Mask

"As iron sharpens iron, so one person sharpens another"
(Proverbs 27:17, NIV).

That is the mantra Erika Hebert strives to live by. She thrives by connecting and bringing people together who can support, encourage, and motivate each other. Erika is committed to improving the well-being of those she serves with compassion and strategies. She holds their feet to the fire by holding them accountable to the goals set forth by them.

Unmasked Authors' Bios

Cheryl Peavy is a Best-Selling Author, Inspirational Speaker, and Inner-Love Coach. Cheryl's main goal is to help women from diverse backgrounds who are faced with traumatic situations in life. Cheryl nurtures and provides them support, resulting in abundant personal growth and transformation in their lives. She is a co-author of *Fabulous New Life II: 20 Beautiful Women* and *I Am Beautiful: The Evolution of Beauty*. She is also the author of *Take All The Time You Need*, an eBook about her personal story of grief and the five stages of grief. Connect with Cheryl at:

Web: www.cherylpeavy.com
Facebook: Cheryl.Peavy.3
Facebook: Cheryl-Peavy
Instagram: CherylPeavy
Twitter: Cheryl_Peavy
www.amazon.com/Cheryl-Peavy

The Woman Behind the Mask

Tamika Quinn is a stroke survivor, veteran, widow, author, Certified John Maxwell Team Speaker, Health & Wellness coach, Mentor, and Owner of Pink Carpet Glam Girl Spa. Tamika has graced faith-based pulpits, corporate training rooms, college campuses, and conference stages sharing her expertise, experience, and enthusiasm for helping people get unstuck and move forward in their life, health, business, and ministry. Tamika has a special place in her heart for helping women avoid having a stroke. Obesity and uncontrolled hypertension were huge factors of Tamika's stroke, so her focus is on educating heart healthiness to women's and children's organizations using her "Fat Girl 2 Glam Girl" program. The self-proclaimed once "fat girl" has lost more than 80lbs and inspires others to make lifestyle changes to get in shape through good nutrition choices. Tamika is also the author of *Worry Free Weight Loss On a Single Momma Budget*. Keep up with Tamika online at www.TamikaQuinn.com.

Unmasked Authors' Bios

Casey Angelle Robinson aka Casey Reed, is a Licensed Clinical Social Worker living in Lafayette, Louisiana, raising her four-year-old son, Nicolas James. Casey received a Master's Degree in Social Work from Louisiana State University, and has been practicing in the field of social work for the past 11 years. Casey has worked in various settings including foster care, mental health, and (most recently) in hospice and palliative care. Casey is currently expanding her skills and knowledge to her interests in writing and public speaking, and would eventually like to mentor and teach new Social Workers entering the field. Connect with Casey at:

Email: caseyred7@yahoo.com
Facebook: Casey.A.Robinson.7
Instagram: TheresOnlyOneReed

The Woman Behind the Mask

Mary Reese-Paul is a passionate and spiritual Life Coach and devoted Child of God.

She leads others towards self-discovery and mental liberation with her daily inspiring messages and journey as a Life Coach.

Her ever-present motto is, "Stop placing a question mark where God has placed a period!" It is a mindset that exemplifies how she firmly believes that far too many of us place an emphasis on the "what-ifs" while not giving God the Glory for the 'Yeses' He presents to us in life.

Visit her website:
www.marysowingseeds.com

Atneciv Rodriguez is a Domestic Violence Advocate in Waterbury, CT. She received her Bachelor's Degree in Science with a Minor in Psychology from the University of Bridgeport, as well as a Certificate in Criminal Justice. She has served several years providing crisis intervention to victims. She is a survivor of domestic violence herself. It was then that she realized her purpose in life was to help others through empowerment and self-sufficiency. Ms. Rodriguez has begun her passionate journey in Life Coaching and is writing her own book on Domestic Violence and safety strategies. She has published a workbook called *Courage and Survival* (available on Amazon) that provides basic strategies of safety planning.

Atneciv can be reached through email at
satneciv@yahoo.com
or via her cell phone at 203-982-9990.